A Man's Whirled

EVERY GUY'S GUIDE TO COOKING WITH A BLENDER

Chris Peterson

Simon & Schuster Paperbacks

New York   London   Toronto   Sydney

SIMON & SCHUSTER PAPERBACKS
Rockefeller Center
1230 Avenue of the Americas
New York, NY 10020

First Simon & Schuster paperback edition 2005

SIMON & SCHUSTER PAPERBACKS and colophon are registered trademarks of Simon & Schuster, Inc.

For information about special discounts for bulk purchases,
please contact Simon & Schuster Special Sales at
1-800-456-6798 or business@simonandschuster.com.

Designed by Joel Avirom and Jason Snyder

Manufactured in the United States of America

10   9   8   7   6   5   4   3   2

Library of Congress Cataloging-in-Publication Data

Peterson, Chris.
    A man's whirled : every guy's guide to cooking with a blender / Chris Peterson.
        p.   cm.
    1. Blenders (Cookery) I. Title.
    TX840.B5P488 2005
    641.5'893—dc22   2005049042
ISBN-13: 978-0-7432-7023-6
ISBN-10:   0-7432-7023-1

To my son, Sam—

*I couldn't have done it without your willingness
to at least try just about anything I put in front of you.
You rock.*

Acknowledgments

I'VE DISCOVERED THAT a first recipe book is no small undertaking, and cannot possibly be completed without a strong supporting cast. I owe many people a debt of gratitude, starting with Mary South, who gave me the first boost of confidence to pitch the idea outside of the comfortable confines of her living room. Thanks also to my agent, Jane Dystel, who supported the idea and represented it with a vigor I don't think another agent could have matched. Her indomitable good spirits have been invaluable to me throughout the process. I owe a special thanks to my editor, Sydny Miner, who gave me a most gracious welcome to cookbook publishing. She was generous with her time, attention, and wisdom, and extremely thoughtful with her editorial direction. I know from experience that it's no easy task to edit an editor-turned-writer and I sincerely appreciate her patience and tact. *A Man's Whirled* is better for her edits.

Tasting is sometimes sweet sorrow, and so I must also thank the crew of tasters who were invaluable in giving me honest feedback. They all helped me to tweak the good recipes and gently sent me back to the drawing board when things went south. Many thanks to the Conrads—Liz, Shannon, Piper, and Rita—and to Tina Manis and Bruce Fisher.

Contents

Introduction

MAN DOES NOT LIVE BY MICKEY D'S alone. Or Arby's. Or Pizza Hut, or by the good grace of Mom, or the selections in the frozen food aisle. A man worthy of being called such does not eat beans out of the can and call it dinner, or regularly make a meal out of tortilla chips dipped in cottage cheese. No, there comes a time in every man's life when he has to step up and take responsibility for his own culinary needs. And if you're over twenty-one and single (or married, or divorced, or somewhere in between), that time is now.

It's not just a matter of nutritional survival, either. Part of the measure of a man is his ability to cook. The measure of sophisticated man who will do amazingly well with members of the opposite sex? The ability to cook *really well*.

There just isn't a downside to possessing a little kitchen prowess. You get to impress friends and family. It'll make you ever more popular with the ladies. You'll eat like a king. All you have to do is take the first steps, which admittedly can be hard. Walk down any aisle in Williams-Sonoma and the whole prospect of cooking a meal can seem like a daunting prospect. That's because Williams-Sonoma is for pompous food geeks, not you. For you, there is an easier answer. That answer is this book and a blender.

Yes, a blender.

As any capable man knows, if you're going to do a job right, you need the right tool. When it comes to whipping up delicious meals fast and easy, a blender is the vise-grips of the kitchen, the all-in-one culinary solution. A blender makes cooking simple, quick, and easy. It chops, it grinds, it crushes, it purees—all in a fraction of the time it would take to do those things by hand. No switching of blades. No fussing with settings.

And fun. A blender can actually make cooking fun. You heard me right. Well, not tickets-to-the-Super Bowl fun, but certainly your-team-wins-in-overtime fun. You put many things in one big container, and they get turned into edible stuff almost magically. You get to push buttons and make lots of noise. You can make drinks, dinner, and dessert, all with the same tool! All you need to do is pick the right blender for you, and off you go.

Choosing Your Tool

First, save yourself the embarrassment and steer clear of "smoothie makers" or immersion blenders. The world doesn't need more wimpy tools. This is a blender book. Real men own blenders. You need a blender. So buy a blender. (Unless you already have one. In which case, kudos.)

That said, don't fall into the power trap. Blenders aren't reciprocating saws; you don't need the most powerful one money can buy. Most of today's blenders have enough power to crush ice and circulate a canister full of thick liquid—which is as much as you'll ever need them to do. Any blender with a 300-watt or better motor is going to supply all the power you need.

Whichever blender you go with, certain features are essential. It has to have removable blades. Otherwise—blades being like the inside of your ears—they'll be impossible to get at and impossible to clean. The blender lid should include a removable cap, so that you can pour ingredients in with the top on while the unit is running.

Don't be seduced by stainless steel canisters. They may look sleek, but to be a top-shelf blender chef, you need to see what's going on inside. That leaves plastic and glass. If you're a klutz (c'mon, you know who you are), or if you're planning on having a lot of blended-drink parties on a flagstone patio, stick with plastic. Otherwise, go with a glass canister that will scratch less over time and will be less likely to vibrate during blending. For all the recipes in this book, you want at least a 40-ounce canister, but bigger is better.

Now here's the dirty little secret about blenders. You ready? You only need three speeds. Three. Yeah, you can buy a fancy model with lots of buttons, and it might make you look like you're handling a really complicated piece of equipment. But here's what you do. Label the button on the far left "low." Label the button in the middle "medium." And label the button on the far right "high." Then scrape the labels off the other buttons. Or just make your life easy and buy one with three speeds.

The type of controls you choose are going to affect how easy the blender is to clean. It's hard to wash the areas between push buttons, so flush-mounted buttons or a dial control is usually better. Then, of course, there's the style of the thing.

Blenders come in all shapes, sizes, colors, and finishes. You can get a pretty red one, or a retro chrome one, or a clean white one. But you notice how style is mentioned last here? Regardless of what *Queer Eye for the Straight Guy* may tell you, it's just not manly to be fussing over the color of small electronic appliances. Pick the blender that works best for you and that makes cooking the easy task it should be. Don't ask for color swatches. Just pick one and get it home before you pass out from hunger.

Then flip the page, set yourself up, and get cooking.

CHAPTER 1

Rookie Playbook: The Kitchen Basics

It all comes back to those days in Boy Scouts and that memorable motto: "Be prepared." You wouldn't try to restore a vintage Harley with a screwdriver and a saw and you can't expect to start cooking real meals when all you've got is a can opener and a pot you picked up at a yard sale. Truth is, even with the world's best blender, you're going to need a few other essentials to make memorable chow. But don't panic—the right equipment and supplies don't need to break the bank and they'll make any cooking you do easier and more enjoyable.

Start by compiling a small collection of essential bakeware and cookware. The simple man's kitchen is equipped with cast iron or nonstick aluminum cookware. Cast iron has great heating characteristics but cleanup can be a pain. Choose enameled cast iron if you opt for iron pots and pans, but for our purposes, high-quality aluminum nonstick cooking gear is best. Here's a list of the fundamental pieces, but you might find more complete sets on sale. Pick other individual pieces to suit your cooking style.

> ➤ 10-inch omelet pan

> ➤ 11- or 12-inch skillet with lid

> ➤ 10- or 12-inch grill pan. Like a skillet with raised ribs to grill meat, fish, and fowl.

> ➤ 2½ quart pot with lid

> ➤ Small saucepot with lid. Buy one that is just big enough for melting butter and other small tasks.

> ➤ Baking sheet. Buy a large rectangular version 1 inch deep. It can be used for baking dishes like crème brûlée, and can double as a cookie sheet.

- 9 by 5-inch loaf pan

- Muffin pan

- 9-inch-square by 2-inch-deep cake pan

- 9-inch-round by 2-inch-deep cake pan

- Large rectangular 2-inch-deep baking pan

- 8- or 9-inch springform pan. This is a round cake pan with a detachable ring that forms the sides. After baking, just unlatch the ring and pull it away, leaving the sides of your cakes intact!

Prep's Cool

The process of prepping raw ingredients to go into one of those pots and pans requires its own set of tools:

- Large stainless steel mixing bowl. Simple Rule Number 27: Small amounts can be mixed in a large mixing bowl, but the reverse is not true.

- Set of measuring spoons (1 tablespoon, 1 teaspoon, ½ teaspoon, ¼ teaspoon).

- Set of measuring cups for dry ingredients in ¼-, ⅓-, ½-, and 1-cup increments.

- 2- or 4-cup-capacity measuring cup for liquids. Buy Pyrex.

- Can opener. Splurge. A well-made can opener with smooth action and a comfortable grip makes life soooo much easier.

- Hand grater. Buy one with a medium-fine cutting surface and a comfortable handle. You'll use this for an amazing array of tasks from zesting oranges to shaving chocolate.

- ➤ Peeler

- ➤ Colander. For draining pasta, washed salad greens, and more. Go for a sturdy stainless steel type with a deep basin and comfortable handles.

- ➤ Handheld strainer. Buy a medium size with a fine-mesh basket and a handle that feels good in your grip.

- ➤ Pepper mill. Fresh-ground pepper is an indispensable ingredient and the only type of black pepper you should use in recipes or to flavor salads and other prepared dishes.

A Cut Above

You don't have to watch *West Side Story* to know how important a good knife is. Buy a name-brand starter set, but handle them before buying to make sure they are good quality (poor knives don't hold an edge and make cutting food a risky and frustrating adventure). You can tell a well-made knife by the grip and the weight. The handle should be comfortable in your hand and the knife should be well balanced as you hold it. The blade should be relatively heavy. This basic set will cover all the cutting you'll need to do in the kitchen (measurements may vary slightly, depending on the set you buy).

- ➤ 8- or 10-inch chef's knife

- ➤ 6-inch utility knife

- ➤ Serrated bread knife

- ➤ 4-inch paring knife

- ➤ 5-inch boning knife

> Steel. Any quality knife set comes with a sharpening steel. It looks like a long, round file with a handle. When a knife begins to dull, carefully run it down the steel (or up) with the knife held at about a 20-degree angle to the steel. Repeat four or five times on each side of the blade. If the steel doesn't sufficiently sharpen the knife, you may need the edge renewed by a professional sharpener. In this case, take your entire knife set to a knife shop or a local hardware store that offers sharpening services.

Get in the habit of cleaning your knives immediately after use. Food left on the blade for extended periods can rust or dull the blade. Store knives on a magnetic hanging strip or in a knife block. Stored loose in a drawer, blades will take a beating and dull much quicker than normal.

Serves You Right

Some handy kitchen essentials do double duty as cookware and serving dishes. These must-haves include:

> Ramekins. Buy a set of 4 porcelain ramekins and you'll be amazed how much you use them. The standard measure is 4 ounces, which makes the ramekin ideal for all kinds of single-serving dishes and for holding condiments or dips during snacktime. Ramekins are also a great way to collect and organize ingredients prior to making a recipe.

> Casserole dish. Buy a porcelain dish that is both oven and dishwasher safe. It should be at least 10 inches in diameter, with the straightest sides you can find (that way it can double as a soufflé dish).

Utilitarian Utensils

In addition to flatware—you do have 4 matching spoons, knives, and forks, right?—an elementary set of cooking utensils is a vital addition to your culinary toolbox. A good set of large utensils includes:

> Solid "basting" spoon

> Slotted spoon

> Solid spatula

> Pasta fork

> Ladle

> Two-tined fork

> Tongs. Buy these in stainless steel or go with nylon if you have nonstick pots and pans.

You also need:

> Wooden spoon

> Rubber spatula

Stocking Up

Once you've equipped your kitchen, it's time to set up your pantry. Or it's time to scratch your head and say, "What's a pantry?" Just so we're clear: a pantry is the place you use to store a basic supply of commonly used ingredients, and canned and packaged convenience foods. It can be as simple as a couple of cupboards, a closet fitted with shelves, or even a stand-alone shelving unit in the corner of the kitchen. The important part is that you have one, and you stock it with cooking basics so that you don't have to run out to the store every time you launch into a recipe.

The Spice Is Right

A modest selection of the most-often-used spices is a crucial part of any well-stocked pantry. As a general rule of thumb, buy the smallest quantity of spice you can find, because just like bubble gum, dried spices lose their flavor over time. Store spices in a cool, dark, and dry location.

In case you were wondering when to use dried spices and when to use fresh, you'll notice we've done a pretty tricky thing with the recipes in this book. Where you need to use dried spices, we put the word "dried." Where you need to use fresh, we've put "fresh." Where the fresh version is not generally used, we've just called the spice by name—if in doubt, the spice is dried. Here's the short list of common spices you probably want to keep on hand. Buy additional spices as the need arises.

> ➤ Allspice

> ➤ Basil

> ➤ Cinnamon

> ➤ Cayenne (also sold as "ground red pepper")

> ➤ Cloves

> ➤ Coriander

> ➤ Ginger

> ➤ Lemon pepper (a great substitute for table salt)

> ➤ Mustard

> ➤ Nutmeg

> ➤ Oregano

- ➤ Paprika

- ➤ Parsley

- ➤ Peppercorns (for filling your mill)

- ➤ Rosemary

- ➤ Thyme

- ➤ Pure vanilla extract

Staple Selection

You also need a supply of "staples," those bit-part players in the drama that is any recipe you make. Even though most of these have a significant shelf life, they all eventually go bad. So buy quantities that are reasonable given the amount of cooking you are likely to do.

- ➤ All-purpose flour. Keep it in an airtight container in a cool place. If you only bake once in a while, store it in the refrigerator.

- ➤ Baking powder. The stuff in a small can.

- ➤ Baking soda. That's the box you keep in the refrigerator to keep it from stinking. But don't use that box for cooking; keep a fresh one in your pantry and never confuse it with baking powder.

- ➤ Beans. Keep canned pinto, kidney, and black beans on hand for recipes, salads, and as side dishes.

- ➤ Broth—beef and chicken. Canned versions are ready to go into soups and sauces.

- ➤ Chocolate. Always buy high-quality, name-brand chocolate because the only thing in life that is more disappointing than finding out she loves another is tasting a special treat made with a decidedly unspecial chocolate. The three main types you'll use for sweet treats are powdered cocoa, semisweet chips, and unsweetened bars or blocks.

- ➤ Condiments. Keep backups of all your favorites, including mustard (Dijon and yellow), ketchup, and mayonnaise.

- ➤ Cooking oil. Buy pure canola oil, one of the healthiest.

- ➤ Olive oil. Cold-pressed extra-virgin. There is no substitute.

- ➤ Pastas. Keep them sealed in their boxes or bags until use.

- ➤ Rice. Keep 1 box of Minute Rice and 1 package of Spanish-style yellow rice on hand.

- ➤ Salt.

- ➤ Sugar. Always keep four types on hand: granulated, confectioners', light brown, and dark brown. Keep any sugar in a tightly sealed airtight package—transfer them to a large zipped sandwich bag if need be—and out of direct light or extremes of temperature. Brown and granulated sugars can be frozen.

- ➤ Tomato products. A can each of paste, sauce, crushed, and diced should cover all your cooking needs.

- ➤ Vegetables. Canned corn, green beans, and peas are quick and easy side dishes to any meal.

- ➤ Vinegar. Keep both red wine and white vinegars on hand.

- ➤ Add to this list any other canned goods, such as canned tuna, that you use regularly.

One last word on pantry maintenance: If you were the coach of the Knicks, would you play four quarters with the same five guys? Of course not. In the kitchen, as in basketball, rotation is key. Get in the habit of always placing newly purchased groceries behind the older stuff. This will cut down on spoilage and help to ensure that you're using the best ingredients for the recipes you make.

With your tools and supplies in order, you're ready to go. So pick a recipe, push a button, and make your tastebuds do the happy dance.

CHAPTER 2

Game Day Grub

Modern science hasn't yet proven the connection between TV viewing and the need to snack, but every sports fan knows it exists. Whether it evolved to keep brothers-in-law from providing irritating running commentary, or is just the by-product of really good subliminal advertising, is beside the point. Filling your yap with a stream of good-tasting, no-fuss chow is as much a part of watching sports as the instant replay.

Quite frankly, snacking is the upside to a lack of box seat tickets. Maybe you're not there in person, but at least you have picture-in-picture, TiVo freeze-frame, and access to a menu that would cost a small fortune at the stadium.

The snacks in this section fulfill the essential criteria of true game day grub. First and foremost, they are all compatible with beer. As a matter of fact, the more beer, the better they taste. Second, all are rib-sticking fare that nobody is going to mistake for health food. Last, but certainly not least, all (with a couple exceptions) can be eaten without utensils.

These nonmeal meals are easy and quick—you can make a whole spread during the pregame report. You can customize them to fit the occasion, and you'll find it simple to double or triple any given recipe to meet the needs of your crowd, regardless of size. So choose which game is the picture in the picture, assemble your posse, and dig in.

Gridiron Guacamole

WHY "GRIDIRON"? BECAUSE ESPN DOESN'T show bullfights, and the only guys we want to see in tights weigh 250 pounds and are trying to clothesline other guys in tights. Besides, this tangy avocado dip is the perfect partner to that truckload of tortilla chips you just bought for the game.

WHAT YOU NEED

1 small clove garlic

1 small white onion

1 tablespoon lime juice

1 teaspoon lemon juice

10 to 12 cilantro leaves

1 small slice jalapeño (about ½ teaspoon chopped)

5 to 6 cherry tomatoes

½ teaspoon salt

2 large ripe Haas avocados

WHAT YOU DO

1. Peel garlic and onion, and chop into coarse pieces. Combine in blender with lime juice, lemon juice, cilantro, and jalapeño. Blend on medium for five 2-second bursts, or until well chopped.

2. Cut the tops off the tomatoes and squeeze out the seeds. Add tomatoes and salt to blender.

3. Cut the avocados in half, remove the pits, and use a spoon to scrape the interiors out into the blender.

4. Blend on low for three to five 2-second bursts, or until well mixed but not smooth. Stop and scrape down sides between each burst.

MAKES 4 SMALL SERVINGS TO GO WITH OTHER SNACKS

THE PERFECT SERVE: Sprinkle the guacamole with lemon juice and cover with an airtight seal such as plastic wrap to keep it from browning. Refrigerate until serving.

OUTSTANDING OPTIONS: There are a million ways to make this tortilla-chip favorite, so try your own. Add your favorite hot sauce or a little bit of habanero pepper to give it kick, or more cilantro and lime to give it added bite. You can also use guacamole as much more than a dip—it's great in an omelet. Or whip up an incredible chicken salad by mixing it with grilled and chopped chicken breast.

Breakout Baba Ghannooj

NO, IT'S NOT THE LATEST RAP STAR, it's a tasty eggplant dip. Only the land of the seven-veils dance could produce such a spicy, filling dip out of a tasteless purple gourd. Make it for the weekend parade of games, or keep it in the fridge for any time you need a protein-rich snack.

WHAT YOU NEED

1 medium eggplant

4 small cloves peeled garlic

¼ cup lemon juice

¼ cup tahini (also sold as "tahina" and "tahine")

¼ teaspoon paprika

1 Kalamata olive

1½ teaspoons salt

Lemon wedges

1 tablespoon olive oil

Fresh-ground pepper to taste

WHAT YOU DO

1. Preheat oven to 425°F.

2. Pierce eggplant several times with fork. Bake in oven for 40 minutes. Let cool for at least 15 minutes.

3. Peel and cut into coarse pieces and combine in blender with garlic, lemon juice, tahini, paprika, olive, and salt. Blend on medium for 1 minute or until smooth, stopping as necessary to scrape down sides with spatula.

4. Chill for at least 30 minutes. Serve with lemon wedges, and drizzle olive oil over top of the dip. Grind pepper over the dip as desired.

MAKES 4 SERVINGS WITH OTHER SNACKS, OR 2 SERVINGS AS PART OF A MEAL

THE PERFECT SERVE: Go to the Middle Eastern roots of this dish by combining it with the traditional partner of torn-up chunks of pita bread. Toast the pita for a different texture and flavor, or serve with unsalted crackers.

SHOP TIP: Find tahini in the ethnic food section of your supermarket, or at a Middle Eastern or gourmet food shop.

Super Bowl of Salsa

IF YOU USUALLY BUY YOUR SALSA IN A JAR, you are not living the high life. Go homemade for an authentic taste that will leave your tongue dancing to the mariachi and your pals calling for another round of *cervezas*.

WHAT YOU NEED

1 large white onion

1 small jalapeño

2 scallions, trimmed

2 tablespoons cilantro leaves

1½ teaspoons fresh lime juice

½ teaspoon lemon juice

½ teaspoon olive oil

¼ teaspoon cider vinegar

2 cups canned diced tomatoes

Salt and pepper to taste

WHAT YOU DO

1. Peel onion and remove ends and seeds of jalapeño. Coarsely chop onion, scallions, and jalapeño.

2. Combine onion, scallion, jalapeño, cilantro, and lime juice in blender. Blend for five to seven 2-second bursts, or until well chopped. Add lemon juice, olive oil, and vinegar to blender.

3. Add tomatoes, salt, and pepper. Blend for 3 seconds on low. Then ensure the top is securely sealed on the canister, and shake contents.

4. Let the salsa sit for at least an hour, either in the blender or in a covered bowl in the refrigerator before serving. Serve chilled.

MAKES 2 LARGE SERVINGS

THE PERFECT SERVE: A tasty, chunky homemade salsa deserves sturdy homemade tortilla chips. Make your own by brushing eight to ten 6-inch corn tortillas with canola oil, and cutting them in quarters. Bake the chips on a baking sheet, in an oven set to 425°F. Bake for 5 to 7 minutes per side or until brown and crunchy. Let cool on a plate covered with layers of paper towels and sprinkle with salt to taste.

Game Day Grub

Grand Slam Clam Dip

SIMPLE AND DELICIOUS, THERE'S JUST no way you can help but love this dip. Unless you're allergic to shellfish. Even then it might be worth it.

WHAT YOU NEED

1 small yellow onion

1 tablespoon lemon juice

2 8-ounce packages cream cheese, softened

2 4-ounce cans minced clams

Pinch cayenne

WHAT YOU DO

1. Peel and quarter onion. Combine onion and lemon juice in blender. Blend on high for three 3-second bursts, or until onions are finely chopped.

2. Cut cream cheese into cubes. Add clams, cayenne, and cream cheese to blender, and blend on medium for 1 minute, periodically stopping to scrape down sides.

3. Chill at least 1 hour before serving.

MAKES 4 SERVINGS

THE PERFECT SERVE: If members of the fairer sex are going to be in attendance at your game day feast, spruce up the presentation of this simple dip. Buy a round loaf of bread, cut the top off, and hollow out the center. Toast the chunks of bread you've removed, and set aside. Bake the bread bowl for 10 minutes at 350°F. When cool, fill with the dip and serve along with the toasted bread pieces and chips.

Casbah Hummus

THIS IS THE ORIGINAL PARTY DIP, DATING BACK a couple thousand years. For the ultimate dip experience, serve it up with torn pieces of pita bread (they hold up to the dip better than chips). This game snack even qualifies as good for you, with tons of protein and fiber.

WHAT YOU NEED

2 medium cloves peeled garlic (1 teaspoon if using preminced)

Olive oil

1 16-ounce can chickpeas, drained

⅔ cup tahini

1 teaspoon salt

Pinch cumin

¾ cup lemon juice

WHAT YOU DO

1. Put garlic in blender with a drizzle of olive oil. Blend 5 seconds on high, or until minced.

2. Add chickpeas, tahini, salt, cumin, and lemon juice, and blend 1 minute on medium, or until smooth. Stop periodically and stir mixture with a spatula, so that it blends smoothly.

MAKES 4 SERVINGS AS A DIP WITH OTHER SNACKS

SHOP TIPS: Buy minced garlic in jars to save the pain-in-the-ass job of peeling and chopping it yourself.

THE PERFECT SERVE: Fresh vegetables are perfect for dipping in hummus, but we all know real men aren't rabbits. A better idea might be to serve the dip with warmed (not toasted) pita bread—just rip off a piece, take a dip, and experience a Middle Eastern pleasure second only to the harem.

Big Bad Bagna Cauda

THIS ANCHOVY-GARLIC DIP IS A SALTY trip to hot fat heaven. The name means "hot bath" in Italian, and it's a traditional Christmas stomach-rubbing, warm-you-up favorite in the old country. But don't you wait for signs of Santa—this treat rocks all winter.

WHAT YOU NEED

4 cloves garlic

1 sprig parsley (½ teaspoon chopped)

¾ cup olive oil

6 tablespoons unsalted butter, softened

Pinch cayenne

¼ teaspoon fresh-ground pepper

Pinch paprika

10 to 12 anchovy fillets

WHAT YOU DO

1. Peel and coarsely chop garlic. Cut stems off parsley and combine with garlic in blender. Blend on low for three to five 2-second bursts, or until well chopped.

2. Add olive oil, butter, cayenne, pepper, paprika, and anchovies. Blend on low for 45 to 60 seconds, or until completely mixed.

3. Pour into saucepan and heat on medium for 2 minutes or until hot, stirring occasionally. Serve immediately in a bowl, or pour into fondue pot and keep hot over warmer.

MAKES 4 SERVINGS WITH OTHER SNACKS

THE PERFECT SERVE: Bagna Cauda is rich and salty and needs to be soaked up with something a little tamer. It's traditionally served with crusty country bread and raw vegetables, such as artichoke hearts, mushrooms, radishes, and any color bell pepper.

A MAN'S WHIRLED

Offensive Line Garlic-and-Bean Dip

YOU KNOW HOW IT feels when your team boots that fifty-five-yard field goal in the final four seconds? Well, that's how your tongue is going to feel when it gets a sample of this smooth and tasty dip.

WHAT YOU NEED

1 clove garlic

¼ cup mayonnaise

½ teaspoon grated Parmesan

1½ teaspoons chili powder

¼ teaspoon cayenne

¼ teaspoon salt

Dash pepper

2 cups canned pinto beans

WHAT YOU DO

1. Peel and chop the garlic into coarse pieces. Combine mayonnaise, garlic, Parmesan, and seasonings in blender. Blend on low for 15 seconds, or until well mixed.

2. Slowly add beans, blending on medium for 1 minute, or until smooth. Stop to scrape down sides as necessary.

3. Put in covered bowl and refrigerate for at least 1 hour before serving.

MAKES 2 LARGE SERVINGS

THE PERFECT SERVE: This thick dip calls for a heavy-duty scooping device. Use sturdy tortilla chips or cut French bread into thick slices, toast them, and spread the dip onto the slices.

GOOD GUY ADVICE: When you add a dash or a pinch of seasoning to a recipe, put the spice into your hand first, then drop it into the blender. If you try to do it direct from the spice jar, it's likely to pour too much.

Game Day Grub

Shrimpy's Three-Point Spread

SHRIMP—HOW CAN SOMETHING so small taste so damn good? It's a puzzle we may never figure out, but, then again, some mysteries are better left unsolved. So just leave that one to the marine biologists, pop a brew, and get busy with that dip.

WHAT YOU NEED

1 small yellow onion

1 tablespoon ketchup

½ teaspoon Worcestershire sauce

1 8-ounce package cream cheese, softened

¼ teaspoon garlic salt

¼ teaspoon salt

Dash black pepper

1 4-ounce can tiny shrimp, drained

WHAT YOU DO

1. Peel and chop onion into coarse pieces. Combine in blender with ketchup and Worcestershire sauce. Blend on high for three 3-second bursts, or until onion is minced.

2. Add remaining ingredients except shrimp. Blend on low for 1 to 2 minutes, or until completely smooth. Stop periodically to scrape down mixture.

3. Add shrimp and blend for 3 seconds on low, just enough to mix in the pieces of shrimp.

4. Scoop into bowl and chill for at least 1 hour before serving.

MAKES 4 SERVINGS WITH OTHER SNACKS

THE PERFECT SERVE: This is one rich, sweet dip. To cut the sweetness, serve with lemon wedges, ice-cold beer, and salty, salty chips.

Blue Cheese Vegetable Bath

OKAY, SO YOUR IDEA OF THE vegetable course is the garnish on your steak. Dude, you need your veggies, but to help choke them down, you need something creamy and tasty. A little of this dip and you may just go vegetarian. At least until the third inning, when you start nuking those bacon-wrapped sausages.

WHAT YOU NEED

1 8-ounce package cream cheese, softened

1 scallion, top trimmed

¼ cup whole milk

¼ cup sour cream

½ cup crumbled blue cheese

3 dashes hot sauce

1 teaspoon lemon juice

WHAT YOU DO

1. Cut cream cheese into cubes. Combine scallion and milk in blender and blend on medium for 15 seconds.

2. Combine the rest of the ingredients in the blender.

3. Blend on low for 1 minute, or until smooth, but with chunks of blue cheese showing. Scrape down sides as necessary.

4. Refrigerate for at least 1 hour prior to serving.

MAKES 4 SERVINGS WITH OTHER SNACKS

Curry Crisp Wash

ALL THE CRICKET PLAYERS FROM BENGAL swear by this smooth and spicy mix. Of course, they call chips "crisps," but this dip tastes just as good whatever accent you put on it. But, listen, you don't have to watch a bunch of guys in white pants and sweater vests chasing the wicket; rugby's playing somewhere in your five hundred channels.

WHAT YOU NEED

1 ¼ cups mayonnaise

2 teaspoons curry powder

½ teaspoon dry mustard

2 teaspoons lemon juice

¼ teaspoon lime juice

Dash salt

WHAT YOU DO

1. Blend all ingredients on low for 1 minute.

2. Chill for at least 30 minutes before serving, and keep any leftovers chilled.

MAKES 4 SERVINGS

THE PERFECT SERVE: Chips are the easy solution, but this dip's just as good with fresh-cut vegetables or cold, cooked shrimp.

A MAN'S WHIRLED

Hog-and-Horse Dip

BACON AND HORSERADISH ARE THE FOOD marriage equivalent of Carmen Electra and Dave Navarro. (Except for the part where they have their own reality show.) Just zesty enough to give chips a little zing, one taste of this dip and your faith in marriage will be restored.

WHAT YOU NEED

1 small yellow onion

3 sprigs parsley

1 tablespoon horseradish

1 cup sour cream

¼ cup mayonnaise

½ cup cooked and crumbled bacon (or bacon bits from the jar)

WHAT YOU DO

1. Peel and chop onion into coarse pieces, and chop stems off parsley. Combine in blender and blend on low for 5 to 10 seconds, or until chopped.

2. Add the other ingredients except for bacon, and blend on medium for 1 minute, scraping down sides as necessary.

3. Add bacon and blend 3 to 5 seconds, or just enough to thoroughly mix in pieces. If you prefer, add bacon in step 2, so pieces are finer and integrated into texture of dip.

MAKES 2 LARGE SERVINGS

Game Day Grub

Home Team Chili

IF WINTER SPORTS ARE YOUR THING, YOU CAN either turn up the thermostat or whip up something a little toastier than onion dip. Sure, you can't eat it with your fingers (that's not a dare . . .), but a few coffee mugs and plastic spoons are all you'll need for this natural companion to beers light and dark. Just make sure you have good cross-ventilation.

A MAN'S WHIRLED

WHAT YOU NEED

1 medium yellow onion

2 cloves garlic

2 stalks celery

½ green bell pepper

1 28-ounce can diced tomatoes

1 dash cayenne

1 teaspoon chili powder

1 tablespoon canola oil

1 teaspoon garlic salt

1 pound ground beef

2 16-ounce cans kidney beans

2 teaspoons Tabasco

Salt and pepper to taste

WHAT YOU DO

1. Peel onion and garlic, and chop onion, celery, and green pepper into coarse pieces.

2. Combine onion, celery, garlic, and green pepper with juice from tomatoes in blender. Blend on medium for five 2-second bursts, or until finely chopped.

3. Add tomatoes, cayenne, garlic salt, and chili powder to blender. Stir mixture with spatula, put top on tightly, and shake.

4. Heat oil in saucepan over medium heat, and crumble ground beef in pan. Stir until the meat is browned. Drain the grease from the pan into the empty tomato can.

5. Add blended mixture and beans to saucepan. Add Tabasco and salt and pepper, stir and bring to boil for about 1 minute.

6. Reduce heat, and simmer covered for 1 hour on low, stirring every 15 minutes.

MAKES 4 MEDIUM SERVINGS

OUTSTANDING OPTIONS: Chili is a little like sex: the basic idea is simple but the trick is to develop your own memorable rendition. This version is a bit tame, but feel free to make it as hot as you dare. Add jalapeño (or, if you're truly tough, habaneros) to the veggies before blending. You can also up the ante by doubling the cayenne or adding more toxic hot sauces in place of the Tabasco. Serve with sour cream or sprinkle with Cheddar (unless you've gone atomic on it—in which case serve with a side of Maalox).

SHOP TIPS: Do yourself a favor and buy prechopped vegetables from your local supermarket's salad bar.

GOOD GUY ADVICE: If nobody's ever explained "simmer" to you, man, you have to get out more. Simmering is cooking food just below the boiling point, so that tiny bubbles escape to the surface, but the liquid doesn't break out in a full boil.

Buffalo Bill's Chicken Wings

LIKE PLAYING A PRESEASON game in twenty-five pounds of pads, this sports bar classic is hot, hot, hot. If you can't stand the heat, find some other snack, because these bad boys bring it. Just be glad you aren't the chicken.

A MAN'S WHIRLED

WHAT YOU NEED

2 tablespoons Tabasco or other hot sauce

2 tablespoons canola oil

1 teaspoon paprika

1 pound chicken wings and drums (about 8 to 13 pieces)

1 small yellow onion

1 clove garlic

1 teaspoon cayenne

¼ cup water

⅓ cup tomato sauce

½ cup white vinegar

4 tablespoons salted butter, melted

1 tablespoon fresh lemon juice

½ teaspoon honey

1 tablespoon ketchup

WHAT YOU DO

1. Preheat oven to 350°F.

2. Combine 1 tablespoon Tabasco with canola oil and paprika in blender. Blend for 3 seconds on high.

3. Place wings and drums in large mixing bowl and cover with sauce. Mix until wings are thoroughly coated.

4. Spread chicken on baking sheet, and bake for 45 minutes.

5. Peel onion and garlic and chop onion into coarse pieces. Combine with remaining ingredients in the blender and blend on low for 1 minute or until mix is smooth. Set aside ¼ cup of this marinade.

6. Marinate baked chicken in a covered bowl with the rest of the marinade, for at least 3 hours and as long as overnight.

7. Broil chicken 3 to 4 inches from heat for 5 minutes on each side, turning until brown and crisp and brushing liberally after 2 minutes with reserved marinade.

MAKES ENOUGH FOR 4 WITH OTHER SNACKS

THE PERFECT SERVE: Go traditional with this one, and plate it up with a blue cheese dip (Blue Cheese Vegetable Bath, page 21) and stalks of celery.

Stuffed Gut Mushrooms

IS THERE NOTHING BUTTER AND BACON can't improve? These palate-pleasing gems may not be healthy, but sometimes life is just about the taste. And if taste is a crime, these mushroom delicacies should be doing life.

WHAT YOU NEED

2 sprigs parsley

1 bunch chives

10 to 12 large white mushrooms

½ cup real bacon bits (or crumbled crisp bacon strips)

½ cup bread crumbs

1 teaspoon soy sauce

2 tablespoons lemon juice

½ teaspoon lime juice

1½ sticks salted butter, melted

¼ cup grated Parmesan

WHAT YOU DO

1. Remove stems from parsley and coarsely chop chives. Remove stems from mushrooms and clean mushrooms with a paper towel. Cut ends off stems.

2. Combine mushroom stems, bacon bits, bread crumbs, parsley, chives, soy sauce, lemon juice, and lime juice in blender. Blend on low for 1 minute, stopping periodically to scrape down sides. Add three-quarters of the butter to the blender, leaving the rest in the pan. Blend for three 2-second bursts.

3. Toss mushroom caps with the butter in the pan.

4. Fill the caps with the blended mixture and line them up on a baking sheet. Broil about 4 inches from heat for 5 minutes, or until browned. Remove and immediately sprinkle with Parmesan. Allow to cool for 5 to 10 minutes before serving.

MAKES 6 SERVINGS WITH OTHER SNACKS

GOOD GUY ADVICE: Cleaning mushrooms is a gentle business. Never wash them because the mushrooms will absorb the moisture and become soggy. Use a paper towel or clean dish towel to thoroughly remove dirt from the surface of the mushroom.

Game Day Grub

Homerun Welsh Rarebit

HEY, IF IT'S GOOD ENOUGH FOR A bunch of pub-crawling rugby players, it's definitely good enough for your couch-loving group of lads. Straight from across the pond, this gut-filling, cholesterol-raising cheesy favorite will leave you licking your chops for more.

WHAT YOU NEED

1 cup beer

1 large egg

1½ tablespoons unsalted butter, softened

1 teaspoon Worcestershire sauce

½ teaspoon dry mustard

½ teaspoon salt

¼ teaspoon pepper

Dash Tabasco

Dash cayenne

1 12-ounce package shredded Cheddar cheese

4 slices sourdough bread, toasted

WHAT YOU DO

1. Heat beer in pot, until hot, not boiling.

2. Combine egg, butter, seasonings, and cheese in blender. Start blending mixture and add beer slowly through top.

3. Blend on low for 1 to 2 minutes, or until smooth. Scrape mixture down periodically during blending.

4. Pour over toast and serve.

MAKES 4 SURPRISINGLY FILLING SERVINGS

GOOD GUY ADVICE: Yes, you may be a creative culinary genius, but don't mess with the ingredients or amounts listed in this recipe. Fiddling with the seasonings tends to make the dish too salty to handle, and removing them makes it a bland melted-cheese mess. You feel like experimenting, customize your car.

Shrimp Scampi Grill

FIRE UP THE COALS FOR A TASTY VARIATION on an old Italian standard. The marinade gives these little fellows mouth-watering flavor. But if just one guy says, "Throw another shrimp on the barbie," well, you know what to do with the skewer.

WHAT YOU NEED

8 sprigs parsley

8 scallions, trimmed

5 small cloves peeled garlic

½ cup canola oil

2 tablespoons lemon juice

½ cup dry white wine

½ teaspoon salt

Pepper to taste

2 pounds jumbo shrimp, peeled and cleaned

Lemon wedges

WHAT YOU DO

1. Remove stems from parsley and chop scallions and garlic into coarse pieces.

2. Combine all ingredients except shrimp and lemon wedges in blender. Blend on high for 15 to 20 seconds, or until well mixed and almost smooth.

3. Marinate shrimp in blender canister, or in a separate covered bowl in the refrigerator, for at least 1 hour.

4. Thread shrimp onto skewers and grill about 5 minutes each side or until pink and firm. Serve on a bed of white or yellow rice, with lemon wedges.

MAKES 4 SERVINGS

GOOD GUY ADVICE: Buy cleaned shrimp whenever possible. If you can't find them, you'll have to clean your own. Peel and slice down the back of the shrimp and, under running water, remove the black vein.

Maddog Shish Kebob Marinade

WE ALL KNOW OF SOME weird marriages that just seem to work against all odds. You could say the same about combining soy sauce and brown sugar. But despite its strange combinations, this marinade gives the meat an incredible taste—Maddog is seldom wrong about these things.

WHAT YOU NEED

2 cloves garlic

3 tablespoons canola oil

½ cup soy sauce

2 tablespoons brown sugar

½ teaspoon salt

1 pinch paprika

1 teaspoon ground ginger

1 teaspoon dry mustard

¼ teaspoon fresh ground pepper

Dash cinnamon

1½ pounds top sirloin
(cut into 2-inch pieces)

WHAT YOU DO:

1. Peel garlic and combine with oil in the blender. Blend on high for 5 seconds.

2. Add other ingredients except meat. Blend on low for 30 seconds, or until well mixed.

3. Marinate the meat overnight in a covered bowl placed in the refrigerator.

4. Toss an assortment of cherry tomatoes, green bell pepper quarters, and onion quarters in marinade, and thread onto skewers with sirloin. Grill until meat is cooked to your liking.

MAKES 4 SERVINGS

OUTSTANDING OPTIONS: What's good for a thin piece of meat is good for a big slab of cow. Use the marinade on steaks for straight-up grilling or to flavor up a nice cut of pork. But don't try it on fish.

Armchair QB Quiche

SAY WHAT YOU WILL ABOUT ITS SISSIFIED reputation, few quick dishes fill the bill for finger food like a well-made quiche. And if you've ever made yourself cheesy scrambled eggs, you've got no excuse to diss this dish.

WHAT YOU NEED

1 shallot

4 chives (about ½ teaspoon, chopped)

1¾ cups shredded Italian blend cheese

½ cup shredded Cheddar cheese

4 large eggs

1¼ cups half-and-half

¼ teaspoon salt

¼ teaspoon pepper

Dash Tabasco

¾ cup bacon bits (or 4 slices crispy bacon, crumbled)

1 9-inch pie shell, unbaked

WHAT YOU DO

1. Preheat oven to 375°F.

2. Peel and quarter shallot. Blend with chives on medium for two 2-second bursts.

3. Add cheeses, eggs, half-and-half, and seasonings to blender. Blend on medium for 10 seconds.

4. Sprinkle bacon bits on the bottom of the pie shell. Pour blender mix into shell.

5. Bake for 45 minutes, or until the crust is deep golden brown.

MAKES 4 HEARTY-MAN SERVINGS

THE PERFECT SERVE: Let the dish cool for 10 minutes, then serve warm if you want to hassle with dishes and utensils. Or let it cool completely and eat slices on napkins.

LINEUP SUBSTITUTIONS: You can substitute canned ham, shrimp, or crabmeat for the bacon. If your cholesterol rating looks like a pro bowler's score, swap an egg substitute like Eggbeaters for the eggs, use lean turkey bacon, and use low-fat versions of the cheeses. For variety, shred sharp Swiss cheese to replace the Italian blend, or use a package of shredded mozzarella.

King o' the Sea Crab Cakes

THIS ORIGINAL CRABBY PATTIE (apologies to Sponge Bob) is Neptune's favorite, and the king knows what's what when it comes to seafood. Word of warning though: Between the oversized satellite dish and the smell of these killer snacks frying, don't be surprised when the neighbors come a-knocking.

WHAT YOU NEED

1 large egg

¼ cup mayonnaise

¼ cup half-and-half

1 cup seasoned bread crumbs

½ teaspoon salt

1 teaspoon Worcestershire sauce

Dash Tabasco

¼ teaspoon paprika

1 teaspoon dry mustard

Pepper to taste

½ teaspoon lemon juice

1 pound fresh lump crabmeat

2 tablespoons canola oil

WHAT YOU DO

1. Combine egg, mayonnaise, half-and-half, bread crumbs, seasonings, and lemon juice in blender. Blend on low for 10 seconds, stopping every few seconds to scrape down the mix.

2. Remove mix into bowl. Add crabmeat and combine with your hands, until the crabmeat is well integrated.

3. Form into thin cakes about the size of Mason jar lid.

4. Heat oil in skillet over high heat. Add cakes and fry about 5 minutes on each side, or until crispy and dark golden brown.

5. Place on stack of paper towels on plate, and let cool for 5 minutes. Serve with Time-Out Tartar Sauce (page 33).

MAKES 6 TO 8 CAKES

GOOD GUY ADVICE: God knows, we all love canned foods. The can opener is second only to the blender as indispensable kitchen utensil. But, pal, go the extra expense and buy fresh lump crabmeat, because canned crabmeat is something even cats won't touch.

A MAN'S WHIRLED

Time-Out Tartar Sauce

JERRY LEWIS NEEDED DEAN, COSTELLO needed Abbott, Van Halen needed David Lee Roth, and crab cakes need a sauce that can hold up to all that rich flavor. Full of complex flavors you'll never find in bottled tartar, here's the perfect sauce for all the fruits of the sea.

WHAT YOU NEED

1 small yellow onion

1 small dill pickle

1 hard-boiled egg

1 tablespoon chopped chives

¼ teaspoon dry mustard

1 tablespoon lemon juice

1 cup mayonnaise

1 tablespoon capers

WHAT YOU DO

1. Peel onion and chop pickle and onion into coarse pieces. Peel and quarter egg.

2. Combine pickle, onion, chives, mustard, and lemon juice in blender. Blend on low for three to five 2-second bursts. Add egg and blend on medium for three 2-second bursts.

3. Add mayonnaise and capers and blend on medium for 10 seconds. Chill until serving.

MAKES ABOUT 1½ CUPS TARTAR SAUCE, OR ENOUGH FOR 4 FISH DINNERS

GOOD GUY ADVICE: No man worth his salt wants to be caught weeping like a willow in the middle of his own kitchen, so do your eyes and your pride a favor—before chopping an onion, run cold water over the peeled onion and the blade of your knife. The cold water keeps the onion oils from vaporizing and getting in your eyes.

CHAPTER 3

Date Food

Here's a little secret if you promise not to tell. You know that old saying that the way to a man's heart is through his stomach? That was written by a man. If a woman had the pen in her hand, the saying would be: "Give a princess a feast, and you might just be royally nighted."

It's true. Women like good food every bit as much as guys do. And while they're always up for trying out the latest hot restaurant, no woman can resist a man who can work wonders in the kitchen all by himself. A little culinary expertise makes you a rare beast in the wilds of dating (or the wilds of marriage, for that matter).

The first step in wowing and wooing her is to create a killer menu. Pick a nice starter, a delicious main course, and an over-the-top dessert. Choose different flavors to dominate each course, and make the meal interesting by alternating cold and hot. Stop rolling your eyes, you rube, this is your chance to impress the hell out of her for a lot less than a meal at that swanky joint downtown. And a month from now, she's not going to remember that swanky joint. But you making her a chocolate mousse to die for? *That* she'll remember forever.

And let's not forget that the romance of any romantic meal lies in the setting as well as the food. The greatest meal is only diminished by being served on a coffee table or under a bare lightbulb. Rule one: There is no light like candlelight. Everybody likes your beer sign, but turn it off. Rule two: Use a tablecloth. A *clean* tablecloth. Rule three: Bedsheets do not qualify as tablecloths. Rule four: Find a vase. Find some flowers. Put flowers in vase and put vase on table. If it all seems too much, remember: Set the table, set the scene. Set the scene, and you set the stage for romance.

Awesome Olive Spread

IF ONLY AFFAIRS OF THE HEART WERE as simple and satisfying as this subtle spread. You wouldn't have to wonder what the right answer is to "Does this make me look fat?" So serve her this appetizer and let things get pleasantly complicated from there.

WHAT YOU NEED

2 small cloves garlic

1 cup Kalamata (also sold as "Calamata") olives, pitted

2 teaspoons fresh thyme

2 tablespoons olive oil

Fresh-ground pepper to taste

Splash lemon juice

WHAT YOU DO

1. Peel and coarsely chop garlic. Blend on high for 3 seconds.

2. Add olives, thyme, and olive oil and blend on medium for 30 seconds, or until well chopped and mixed.

3. Sample and blend in pepper and lemon juice to taste, on low for 2 to 5 seconds.

MAKES 2 LARGE SERVINGS

GOOD GUY ADVICE: Even the ever-perfect blender has its drawbacks. In the case of small quantities of taste-intensive spread, the flaw is the cavity beneath the blades, a space that often won't release its bounty. When you want to get every last bite, unscrew the blade assembly from the canister housing, and scoop out your culinary treasure with a knife or small spoon.

THE PERFECT SERVE: This spread is an incredibly versatile culinary performer. It stands alone as a dip with water crackers, torn pieces of French bread, or other partners that let its rich flavors come out. The spread is also a great topping for omelets, scrambled eggs, and all things seafood, from lobster medallions to grilled shark.

Date Food

Smokin' Salmon Spread

BRUNCH IS THE ULTIMATE CASUAL DATE, and no brunch is complete without a chewy, fresh bagel and a "schmear" of cream cheese. Make the casual moment memorable with a rich and creamy dip garnished with a Mimosa or four.

WHAT YOU NEED

½ small yellow onion

2 ounces smoked or cured salmon

1 8-ounce package cream cheese, softened

2 teaspoons lemon juice

2 teaspoons capers

WHAT YOU DO

1. Peel and chop onion in half, and blend on medium for three 2-second bursts, or until finely chopped.

2. Tear salmon into coarse pieces, tossing the pieces into the blender. Cut cream cheese into cubes and add to blender, with lemon juice. Blend on low for 1 minute, scraping down sides as necessary.

3. Add 1 teaspoon capers and blend on low for about 5 seconds, or until the capers are blended into the mix.

4. Chill in covered bowl for at least 30 minutes before serving. Sprinkle remaining capers over top of spread when serving.

MAKES 4 SERVINGS

THE PERFECT SERVE: Salmon spread and bagels beg to be set up with that other brunch favorite—the Mimosa. Champagne cocktails show that you have a little wordly style, without the twelve-step looks you get when you serve morning beer. Mimosas are as simple as they are tasty. Just combine equal parts of chilled brut champagne and cold orange juice (champagne first) in a tall champagne flute. Tell her the bubbles remind you of her sparkle. Go ahead, tell her.

Susan's Super Simple Soufflé

SUSAN'S NOT SIMPLE, IT'S her soufflé that's simple. And super. She's super. The soufflé is super. You can make a simple super supper for someone sweet like Susan.

WHAT YOU NEED

1 clove garlic

1 cup whole milk

1 8-ounce bag shredded Cheddar cheese

4 tablespoons salted butter, softened

4 tablespoons all-purpose flour

5 eggs, separated

½ teaspoon salt

½ teaspoon fresh-ground pepper

Dash cayenne

WHAT YOU DO:

1. Preheat oven to 375°F.

2. Peel and chop garlic into coarse pieces. Blend on medium for three 1-second bursts.

3. Add all other ingredients except egg whites to blender. Blend on medium for 30 seconds, or until smooth.

4. Empty blender into saucepan and stir over low heat for 1 to 2 minutes, until thick.

5. Clean blender canister and blend egg whites on high for 2 minutes. Fold egg whites into sauce.

6. Pour into greased 2-quart baking dish. Bake for 45 to 50 minutes, or until deep golden brown and puffed. Let cool for 10 minutes before serving.

MAKES 4 SERVINGS

THE PERFECT SERVE: The sad truth is, my friend, soufflés fall. That's a fact of life, so don't be surprised when yours does. It's not going to affect the taste.

Date Food

Tantalizing Goat Cheese Timbales

THINK OF IT AS A MINI goat cheese soufflé. Or maybe think of it as the irresistible offering you set before her, that says, "I care that only the finest food touches your pristine lips, in the hope that at some moment, I might." Or maybe it's just a delectable way to make it from cocktails to main course.

WHAT YOU NEED

½ pound goat cheese, well softened

2 tablespoons unsalted butter, softened almost to melting

4 large eggs

4 large egg whites

2 tablespoons grated Parmesan

2 teaspoons fresh thyme

½ teaspoon fresh tarragon

¼ teaspoon paprika

Dash lemon juice

½ teaspoon fresh-ground pepper

¼ teaspoon salt

WHAT YOU DO

1. Preheat oven to 350°F. Grease individual-serving ramekins well (sides and bottom).

2. Combine goat cheese and butter in blender and blend on medium for three 2-second bursts, or until mostly blended.

3. Add the remaining ingredients and blend on medium for 1 minute, or until smooth. You'll need to stop, scrape down, and stir the mix at least twice during blending.

4. Pour mix into ramekins. Place ramekins in baking pan and add warm water to the pan so that it comes halfway up the outside of the ramekins. Bake 25 to 30 minutes, or until a knife inserted in the timbale comes out clean.

5. Let cool for 5 minutes, then very carefully scrape around the edges and lightly pry the timbale out of the ramekin.

MAKES 4 TO 6 SERVINGS

THE PERFECT SERVE: Delicious as it may be, this dish looks a little plain on the plate. Sprinkle chives or caviar over top before serving, and surround with toast points. Make toast points by cutting the crust off a slice of white bread, then cutting it in an *X* to make four triangles. Toast them on a baking sheet in an oven set to 425°F for 3 to 5 minutes, or until golden brown. For a more complete presentation, lightly toss baby spinach leaves in Mambo Italiano Dressing (page 76) and arrange on a saucer. Sprinkle with roasted pine nuts and place the timbale in the center.

GOOD GUY ADVICE: Ramekins are small porcelain baking pots ideal for making single servings of baked foods, like this recipe, and many desserts. They can also be handy for holding small amounts of ingredients as you prepare to make a recipe. If you don't have a set of ramekins, get yourself out to a store that sells cooking gear and stock up.

Sumptuous Shrimp Roll

IT'S A GOOD BET NO GUY HAS EVER MADE her shrimp rolls before—so tell her that takeout's for self-centered mugs who don't really care what their date eats. And then whip up these sensational culinary delights that'll leave her wondering, "What can't he do?"

WHAT YOU NEED

Pancakes

2 large eggs

½ cup water

¼ teaspoon salt

½ cup all-purpose flour

2 tablespoons canola oil

Filling

½ medium carrot

½ stalk celery

1 scallion

1 teaspoon salt

½ teaspoon fresh-ground ginger

Fresh-ground pepper to taste

1 teaspoon granulated sugar

1 4-ounce can tiny shrimp

1 tablespoon canola oil, plus additional for frying

WHAT YOU DO

Pancakes

1. Blend eggs on high for 5 seconds. Stop and remove 2 tablespoons and set aside in a cup.

2. Add water, salt, and flour to blender. Blend on medium 5 to 10 seconds, or until smooth.

3. Heat 2 tablespoons canola oil in 9-inch skillet over medium heat. Pour in just enough batter to cover the bottom, rolling it around to make the coating as thin as possible.

4. Cook on 1 side until golden, about 3 minutes. Turn out on towel, cooked side up, to cool.

5. Repeat with the rest of the batter. Should make 4 to 5 pancakes.

Filling

1. Scrub carrot, and chop carrot, celery, and scallion into coarse pieces. Combine in blender and blend on high for 3 to 5 seconds, or until finely chopped.

2. Add seasonings, sugar, shrimp, and 1 tablespoon oil. Blend for five 2-second bursts, or until well mixed.

A MAN'S WHIRLED

3. Scoop about 1 tablespoon of mixture into the center of each pancake. Even out the amount in each pancake before rolling. Roll pancakes, folding in the sides.

4. Moisten the edges of the pancakes with reserved egg, and seal with a pinch. Chill for at least 1 hour.

5. Heat 1 inch of oil in heavy pan on medium-high heat for 2 minutes. Fry rolls, turning them until they are a dark golden brown all around, about 3 minutes each side.

6. Remove rolls to drain on paper towels and let cool for at least 10 minutes. Serve with mustard sauce or soy sauce.

MAKES 4 TO 5 EGG ROLLS

GOOD GUY ADVICE: The recipe here makes traditional thin and dense pancakes. For lighter, healthier, and fluffier pancakes, cook them without oil in a nonstick skillet.

Enchanté Vinaigrette

THE FIRST STEP IN SHOWING HER YOU'RE a sophisticated kind of guy is not insulting her tastebuds with bottled salad dressing. When the meal counts, keep the store-bought stuff in the fridge and bring on this incredibly tasty dressing. She'll be enchanted.

WHAT YOU NEED

½ shallot, peeled and trimmed

1½ tablespoons Dijon mustard

2½ teaspoons red wine vinegar

4 tablespoons extra-virgin olive oil

½ teaspoon fresh thyme

½ teaspoon lemon zest

Salt and pepper

WHAT YOU DO

1. Blend shallot on high for 3 seconds. Add other ingredients to blender and blend on high for 20 seconds.

2. Serve immediately or refrigerate until use.

MAKES ENOUGH DRESSING FOR 6 SALADS

GOOD GUY ADVICE: Don't be confused by zest. It's not a bar of soap, it's the grated outer portion of the peel on a piece of citrus fruit. Grate just enough to get the surface with the oils and aroma, leaving the bitter white pith behind. The handiest way to do this is with a simple hand zester/grater, best known by the brand name Microplane. This type of grater makes quick work of any modest task, from zesting a lemon to grating Parmesan.

Hail Caesar (and Caligula) Dressing

ONE SURE WAY TO harsh her mellow is to start that special meal off with a lump of iceberg doused in a store-bought dressing. Might as well wear sweatpants and a torn Metallica T-shirt. Don't be a schlub, get things going the right way with a classic Caesar salad featuring this rich and tasty dressing.

WHAT YOU NEED

3 tablespoons extra-virgin olive oil

1 large clove peeled garlic

3 anchovy fillets

2 tablespoons freshly grated Parmesan

1½ tablespoons lemon juice

½ teaspoon red wine vinegar

1 large egg

1 tablespoon Dijon mustard

1 teaspoon Worcestershire sauce

Salt and fresh-ground pepper to taste

WHAT YOU DO

1. Combine a splash of olive oil, garlic, and anchovy fillets in blender. Blend on high for 3 seconds, or until finely chopped.

2. Add the rest of the ingredients and blend on medium until thoroughly combined—about 10 seconds. Store in refrigerator until ready to serve.

MAKES ENOUGH DRESSING FOR 2 LARGE SALADS

THE PERFECT SERVE: Caesar salad is traditionally made with fresh, crisp romaine (hearts of romaine are a great choice) and high-quality seasoned croutons. Toss the romaine and croutons with the dressing before serving, but just coat the leaves—don't saturate them. Serve garnished with anchovies (unless you or your date has a revulsion to the little fellows).

GOOD GUY ADVICE: You should never serve food containing raw egg to pregnant women, infants, or the elderly (or anyone with a compromised immune system). If you are concerned about the quality of the eggs you buy (salmonella in eggs comes from the chickens being kept in unsanitary conditions), substitute 1 teaspoon of mayonnaise for the egg.

Date Food

Say Oui, Mon Chérie! Onion Soup

A FAKE FRENCH accent may just irritate her, but a nice bowl of hearty French soup will satisfy her soul as well as her stomach. Save this one for chilly nights, when you spin an Edith Piaf CD and pretend you're wooing her in sight of the Eiffel Tower. But lose the beret—that's just going too far.

WHAT YOU NEED

2 large yellow onions

¼ stalk celery

4 tablespoons salted butter

½ cup Marsala

2 cups canned beef broth

8 to 10 slices French baguette

¼ cup shredded Parmesan cheese

WHAT YOU DO

1. Peel and quarter onions. Chop celery into coarse pieces.

2. Blend 2 onion quarters at a time on medium for three 2-second bursts, or until uniformly chopped in pieces about the size of a pencil eraser. Blend celery for two 2-second bursts, or until finely chopped. Combine in saucepan with butter.

3. Simmer on medium heat for about 15 minutes, or until the onions begin to brown and the pan is slightly glazed.

4. Add Marsala and scrape the bottom of the pan to free the glaze. Cook on high heat for 5 minutes.

5. Add beef broth and reduce to medium heat. Simmer for 20 minutes. Meanwhile, toast slices of baguette.

6. To serve, fill soup bowls two-thirds full and place toasted bread slices on top of soup. Cover with layer of Parmesan and put under broiler for 3 to 5 minutes, or until melted cheese forms a crust and begins to char slightly.

MAKES 2 LARGE SERVINGS

A MAN'S WHIRLED

Summer Sparkling Soup

A LITTLE BUBBLY AND THE SWEET FRUIT of summer combine to make a memorable light and refreshing meal for a hot, balmy night. The soup, like her presence, can be a little intoxicating. A touch of champagne usually leads to more champagne. And who knows where that might lead?

WHAT YOU NEED

2 medium cantaloupes

½ honeydew melon

Zest of 1 orange

1 teaspoon lemon juice

¼ cup honey

1 split brut champagne

WHAT YOU DO

1. Skin, seed, and chop the melons into coarse chunks. Place in a bowl with other ingredients, mix around for a minute, and put covered in the refrigerator to chill for 2 hours.

2. Scoop fruit and liquid into the blender and blend on medium for 1 minute, or until completely smooth and there is no separation of ingredients. Serve immediately.

MAKES 6 SERVINGS

THE PERFECT SERVE: All cold, sweet soups should be served in chilled bowls, although you can add a unique touch by serving this one in the chilled, hollowed-out cantaloupe halves. Garnish with a mint sprig.

GOOD GUY ADVICE: Buy already-cut melons in pint or quart containers from your local grocery store. Stores usually cut the ripest melons. This soup is best made in the middle of summer, when the melons are in season.

Red Velvet Roasted Pepper Soup

A SMOOTH, SMOOTH SOUP is a great dish to have in your culinary bag of tricks, and this one is the smoothest of all. Smooth like velvet. Smooth like Sinatra. Speaking of which, you do have chip-free soup dishes for this stuff, right?

WHAT YOU NEED

1 small yellow onion

3 cloves garlic

½ stalk celery

4 tablespoons olive oil

½ medium Idaho potato, peeled

1 12-ounce jar roasted red peppers

¼ teaspoon paprika

½ teaspoon salt

½ teaspoon fresh-ground pepper

4 cups water

1 tablespoon lemon juice

¼ teaspoon hot sauce

WHAT YOU DO

1. Peel onion and garlic and chop into coarse pieces. Chop celery into coarse pieces. Blend all three on high for three 2-second bursts. Combine in saucepan with olive oil.

2. Chop potato into coarse pieces and blend on high for three to five 2-second bursts, or until well chopped. Add to saucepan. Cook on medium heat for 10 minutes, or until onions are soft.

3. Add red peppers, paprika, salt, and pepper. Cook for 2 minutes, and add water. Bring to a boil.

4. Reduce to simmer and cook for 30 minutes.

5. Remove soup from heat and let cool. Spoon into blender. Blend on medium for 20 to 30 seconds, or until smooth.

6. Return to saucepan, and stir in lemon juice and hot sauce. Heat for 3 to 5 minutes and serve. Garnish with basil leaves or a swirl of sour cream.

MAKES 2 LARGE SERVINGS

Chillin', Dillin', and Fillin' Cold Cuke Soup

A COLD SOUP DOESN'T HAVE TO WAIT for a hot night. Sometimes it's a way to change the pace of a meal—kind of like a changeup before a fastball. This one goes down easy, but has a little bite.

WHAT YOU NEED

4 cucumbers

4 scallions

1 cup cold vegetable stock

2 cups plain yogurt

½ cup sour cream

½ teaspoon white vinegar

¼ cup lemon juice

2 tablespoons fresh dill

Dash ground ginger

Salt and pepper to taste

WHAT YOU DO

1. Peel and seed the cucumbers. Coarsely chop the scallions and cucumbers, and combine in the blender.

2. Add the cold vegetable stock and blend on medium until the vegetables are well chopped.

3. Add yogurt, sour cream, vinegar, and lemon juice and blend 15 to 20 seconds on medium, or until smooth. Add dill and ginger and blend for 5 seconds on medium.

4. Chill the soup for at least 1 hour. Taste before serving and mix in salt and pepper, or more lemon juice, as desired.

MAKES 4 MODEST SERVINGS

GOOD GUY ADVICE: You can find canned vegetable stock—and other stocks, for that matter—in the soup aisle of your supermarket.

Vixen's Veal Parm

SOME OCCASIONS CALL FOR LIGHT AND delicate soups or salads, but once in a while a man needs to serve up heartier fare. Keep it simple—two candles, a good bottle of Chianti, torn chunks of country bread, and this robust meal on a plate. Recommended by four out of five Mafia dons.

WHAT YOU NEED

1 ½ cups bread crumbs

½ cup finely grated Parmesan cheese

½ teaspoon dried oregano

½ teaspoon dried thyme

¼ teaspoon dried parsley

¼ teaspoon salt

¼ teaspoon fresh-ground pepper

2 large eggs

1 tablespoon water

1 pound thin veal cutlets

1 clove garlic

½ cup extra-virgin olive oil

1 8-ounce can tomato sauce

½ pound mozzarella, sliced

Fresh basil leaves

WHAT TO DO

1. Preheat oven to 325°F.

2. Combine bread crumbs, Parmesan, and spices in blender. Blend on high for 20 to 30 seconds. Put aside in large, flat-bottomed bowl or plate with lip.

3. Combine eggs and water in blender. Blend on low for 5 seconds.

4. Put veal in blender with the top on (check for tight seal). Shake blender canister until the veal cutlets are thoroughly coated in egg mixture.

5. Remove cutlets, one at a time, with tongs or fork. Flip in crumb mixture until completely coated.

6. Peel and coarsely chop garlic. Combine olive oil and garlic in blender, and blend on low for three 2-second bursts.

7. Heat oil-and-garlic mixture in large skillet over medium heat. Place cutlets in pan and cook, about 3 to 5 minutes on each side, or until coating is dark golden and crusty.

8. Put splash of tomato sauce on top of each cutlet, cover with sliced mozzarella, and bake in oven for 10 minutes, or until cheese is melted. Top each with a basil leaf and serve.

THE PERFECT SERVE: Veal parm is pretty much a meal on its own, but it's traditionally served with a small pile of spaghetti coated with a little of the tomato sauce from the parm.

GOOD GUY ADVICE: Buy the thinnest veal cutlets you can find. If you can't find really thin cutlets, buy thicker cutlets, sandwich each cutlet between sheets of waxed paper, and pound flat with a heavy skillet or kitchen mallet. Funny how sometimes cooking is just like working on your car.

51

Date Food

Cupid's Chicken Satay with Peanut Dipping Sauce

OH, THAT CUPID. WHO KNEW HE was Indonesian? This is the recipe he uses when he runs out of arrows, and it makes any Valentine's Day a culinary affair. Or, for that matter, any culinary affair into a Valentine's Day.

WHAT YOU NEED

Satay

6 cloves garlic

¼ cup sesame oil

3½ teaspoons coriander

¼ teaspoon cumin

4 teaspoons light brown sugar

2 teaspoons fresh-ground black pepper

1½ teaspoons salt

½ cup soy sauce

4 teaspoons fresh-ground ginger

½ teaspoon lemon zest

2 tablespoons lime juice

2 pounds thin boneless chicken breasts

WHAT YOU DO

Satay

1. Peel and quarter garlic. Blend with sesame oil on medium for three 2-second bursts, or until finally chopped.

2. Add remaining ingredients except for chicken. Blend on high for 1 minute.

3. Cut chicken in quarters if skewering, or leave whole to grill as cutlets. Combine marinade and chicken in container with lid.

4. Marinate in refrigerator for at least 2 hours, but up to 12.

5. Grill on skewers or as cutlets, until thoroughly cooked. Serve with Peanut Dipping Sauce.

Peanut Dipping Sauce

1 clove garlic

2 tablespoons soy sauce

2 tablespoons fresh lime juice

¼ teaspoon lemon juice

⅓ cup creamy peanut butter

1 teaspoon sugar

Dash cayenne

Dash Tabasco

⅓ cup water

Peanut Dipping Sauce

1. Peel garlic, and combine with soy sauce and lemon and lime juices in blender. Blend on high for 10 seconds.

2. Add remaining ingredients and blend on high for 45 seconds.

MAKES 4 SERVINGS

OUTSTANDING OPTIONS: For a different texture in the dipping sauce, use chunky peanut butter.

SHOP TIPS: Here's something you might not know—there are several different types of soy sauce that are made from different ingredients and have subtle differences in taste. Shoyu is a mixture of soy beans and wheat, tamari is made purely from soy beans. Substitute shoyu for the soy sauce in the marinade to give it a more complex taste.

Date Food

Summer Night Shrimp Creole

NO PLACE CAPTURES THE passion and spice of life quite like New Orleans, and no dish captures New Orleans quite like spicy Shrimp Creole. So spin that Zydeco CD and sit her down to a meal that'll get her heart thumping so quick she'll want to re-create the best scenes from *Body Heat*.

WHAT YOU NEED

1 tablespoon dried thyme

1 teaspoon paprika

½ teaspoon cayenne

Heavy dash salt

Fresh-ground black pepper

3 shallots

6 cloves garlic

1 medium yellow onion

3 tablespoons olive oil

1 jalapeño

2 stalks celery

½ cup fresh parsley (about 10 sprigs)

½ cup dark rum

1 cup clam juice

1 28-ounce can crushed tomatoes

1 6-ounce can tomato paste

WHAT YOU DO

1. Combine the thyme, paprika, cayenne, salt, and about a teaspoon of ground black pepper in blender. Blend on high for 3 seconds. Set aside.

2. Peel and coarsely chop shallots, garlic, and onion. Combine shallots and garlic in blender with a drizzle of olive oil and blend on medium for three 2-second bursts, or until chopped.

3. Add rest of olive oil and onion to blender. Blend on medium for three to five 2-second bursts, or until chopped. Empty blender into large saucepan, and cook over medium heat.

4. Cut and remove ends and seeds from jalapeño. Coarsely chop the celery and remove stems from parsley. Combine jalapeño, celery, and parsley in blender, and blend on high for three 2-second bursts or until finely chopped. Add to saucepan.

5. Add spice blend to saucepan. Cook on medium heat for about 5 to 10 minutes more, or until onions are clear. Add rum and clam juice. Bring to boil for 2 minutes.

Juice of 4 limes (or use ¼ cup bottled lime juice)

1 teaspoon of your favorite hot sauce

1 16-ounce bag deveined, cooked, frozen medium shrimp

1 8-ounce box Spanish-style yellow rice

6. Add tomatoes, tomato paste, lime juice, and hot sauce. Reduce to simmer.

7. Simmer for 45 minutes, then add shrimp (don't defrost them). Simmer for 15 minutes more.

8. Prepare yellow rice according to box or bag directions. Spoon Creole over rice and serve hot, hot, hot.

MAKES 4 SERVINGS

GOOD GUY ADVICE: Make sure you wash your hands regularly when handling hot peppers and hot sauce. You touch your eyes more often then you think, and if your fingers have any pepper juice or hot sauce on them, you're going to learn what it feels like to be in the middle of Mardi Gras crowd control when the gas canisters start flying.

OUTSTANDING OPTIONS: This is spicy with a capital *S*. If you or your date can't handle hot food, you can tone the recipe down a few notches by doing without the jalapeño and cutting back on the cayenne and hot sauce.

Date Food

Monkfish Grill + Boy

FLAME IS YOUR FRIEND. YOU TAME THE flame. You are Master of the Flame. Monkfish— the poor man's lobster—dares you to show it the flame. So fire up your grill, say "Dance flame, dance," and show her how the Master of the Flame turns a simple fish into a blaze-worked culinary masterpiece.

A MAN'S WHIRLED

WHAT YOU NEED

2 cloves garlic

⅓ cup sesame oil

½ teaspoon white vinegar

2 tablespoons grated fresh ginger

½ tablespoon cayenne

1 teaspoon coarse-ground pepper

¼ teaspoon garlic salt

⅓ cup soy sauce

1 tablespoon honey

1 pound monkfish fillets

2 red bell peppers

2 green bell peppers

1 large yellow onion

WHAT YOU DO

1. Peel and halve garlic. Combine with oil and vinegar in blender and blend on high for 5 seconds.

2. Add seasonings, soy sauce, and honey to blender. Blend on high for 15 seconds.

3. Cut monkfish into 1½-inch pieces. Seed peppers and peel onion, and cut all into quarters.

4. Put fish, peppers, and onion into blender canister and shake to coat. Pour contents into shallow container with cover.

5. Marinate for 2 to 12 hours in refrigerator.

6. Thread skewers with fish, peppers, and onions, and grill for 3 to 5 minutes, or until fish is flaky. Serve on bed of white rice.

MAKES 4 SERVINGS

THE PERFECT SERVE: This is a simple dish that needs only a few thick lemon wedges and a nice Sauvignon Blanc to make a memorable meal.

Perfect Pesto

THIS CLASSIC SAUCE DATES BACK TO MEDIEVAL EUROPE, where Italian princes shared it with their mistresses. Be a prince yourself, and offer this rich, garlicky taste sensation to the woman of your dreams.

WHAT YOU NEED

2 cups fresh basil leaves

½ cup extra-virgin olive oil

2 medium peeled garlic cloves

1 teaspoon salt

Dash finely ground black pepper

2 tablespoons roasted pine nuts

½ cup freshly grated Parmesan

½ teaspoon grated Pecorino cheese

WHAT YOU DO

1. Combine basil, ¼ cup olive oil, garlic, salt, and pepper in blender. Blend on medium for three 2-second bursts, scraping down the sides between bursts.

2. Add the remaining olive oil and pine nuts and blend on low for 10 to 20 seconds, until the nuts are finely chopped. Stop and scrape down the sides as necessary.

3. Add cheeses and blend on low for 1 minute.

MAKES 4 SERVINGS

THE PERFECT SERVE: Pesto is your paisan when it comes to winning a woman's undying admiration. It can be poured over hot pasta (especially ravioli), used as a dip for torn hunks of old-country crusty bread, or as a delicious dressing on a simple summer salad of fresh vine tomatoes and mozzarella. Add a few glasses of mellow Barolo—and chum, that's amore.

OUTSTANDING OPTIONS: This is a pretty balanced version of the sauce, so play around with it as you like to adjust it to your taste. Add more garlic for a stronger bite, or more basil for a richer herb taste.

GOOD GUY ADVICE: Mom was right, cleanliness is next to godliness. Especially in cooking. Whenever you use fresh leafy greens or herbs—such as the basil in this recipe—wash and dry them thoroughly. Rinse under cold running water, and either dry them in a lettuce spinner (a covered bowl with a spinning colander inside) or between several layers of paper towel.

Paloma Blanco Clam Sauce

SAVE THE CREAM FOR YOUR coffee. This white clam sauce relies on the delicate and sophisticated coupling of the clams' own juice with the butter and wine. Cook the angel hair pasta just right, and you may be on your way to some sophisticated coupling of your own.

WHAT YOU NEED

2 small yellow onions

5 cloves garlic

4 tablespoons salted butter

½ teaspoon salt

1 teaspoon fresh-ground pepper

2 tablespoons fresh parsley (about 6 sprigs)

2 10-ounce cans whole clams

½ cup dry white wine (preferably Sauvignon Blanc)

WHAT YOU DO

1. Peel onions and garlic and chop into coarse pieces. Combine in blender and blend on high for three 2-second bursts.

2. Heat butter, garlic, and onions in saucepan over medium heat for about 5 minutes, or until onions are soft. Add salt and pepper.

3. Chop stems off parsley and blend on high for two 3-second bursts, or until finely chopped. Add to saucepan.

4. Drain clams and set juice aside. Add clams to saucepan. Add white wine. Bring to a boil, and reduce to a simmer. Simmer for about 5 minutes.

5. Add clam juice and simmer for 10 to 15 minutes, or until sauce reduces by about a third.

6. Mix clam sauce into large bowl of cooked angel hair pasta (about half a pound of fresh pasta). Serve immediately.

MAKES 4 SERVINGS

GOOD GUY ADVICE: One sure way to ruin a great sauce is to make a pile of sticky, overcooked pasta. Avoid that tragedy by cooking your pasta in a large pot with lots of water—4 quarts or more for every pound of pasta. When the water begins to boil, add a tablespoon of salt and then bring it back to a boil before tossing in the pasta. Stir often while cooking, which should take 7 to 10 minutes. Once the pasta is cooked so that it is still slightly firm when you bite it, drain it immediately, and mix with the sauce in a bowl. Don't let it sit. As a general rule of thumb, a 1-pound package of pasta will feed 4 people.

Baby's Béarnaise

YOU GOT YOUR BABY, AND SHE WANTS A SAUCE like they make in great restaurants, something that a guy in a big puffy white hat would send out on a nice piece of steamed fresh fish. That's what baby wants, so that's what baby gets.

WHAT YOU NEED

2 large egg yolks

1 tablespoon lemon juice

1 teaspoon white wine vinegar

1 teaspoon fresh tarragon leaves

1 tablespoon fresh parsley (about 3 sprigs)

1½ sticks salted butter, melted

WHAT YOU DO

1. Combine all ingredients except butter in the blender, and blend on low for 5 seconds.

2. With the blender running, slowly add a third of the butter in a dripping, steady stream.

3. Change to high speed and very slowly add the remaining butter. Serve immediately.

MAKES 4 SERVINGS

THE PERFECT SERVE: Béarnaise is a traditional and versatile sauce that complements steak, fish of all types, poultry, and veal. It can even be a great sauce for steamed veggies.

Hot-for-Her Hollandaise

WHAT KIND OF MAN SLAVES OVER A delicate sauce? Her kind of man. Show her how much you care by serving the sauce of kings (and the king of sauces), but don't let on that it didn't really require any slaving—the illusion is all part of the allure.

WHAT YOU NEED

2 large egg yolks

2 tablespoons lemon juice

1 stick unsalted butter, melted

¼ teaspoon salt

Dash cayenne

Dash white pepper

WHAT YOU DO

1. Combine yolks and lemon juice in blender. Blend on low for 3 seconds.

2. With the blender running, pour the butter into the center of blades, very slowly—in a thin stream slightly more than a series of drops. Leave blender running.

3. Add spices. Blend on low for 15 to 20 seconds more, until the sauce is thick and smooth.

4. Serve immediately, or keep it in a bowl placed in a pan of warm water until ready to serve. What you don't use, throw out—hollandaise doesn't keep.

MAKES 2 GENEROUS SERVINGS

THE PERFECT SERVE: This is the platoon player of sauces. It works as well over an omelet as it does spread on steamed asparagus or a nice fillet of sole.

GOOD GUY ADVICE: There's no big trick to separating an egg. Just carefully crack it in half, and pour the yolk back and forth between the halves of the shell until all the egg white drips away. If that's a little too much finesse for you, just break the egg softly into a bowl, and gently scoop out the yolk, letting the egg white drip away between your fingers.

A MAN'S WHIRLED

The Morning-After Omelet

SHE WAS INCREDIBLE. SHE ROCKED your world. You're head over heels. You want to sing her a song of love and devotion everlasting. You've heard your voice—stick to the cooking and whip up a gourmet masterpiece that will really show her how much you care.

WHAT YOU NEED

½ cup lobster meat (about half a large lobster tail)

3 tablespoons unsalted butter

4 large eggs

1 tablespoon half-and-half

½ cup shredded Monterey Jack cheese

2 tablespoons crème fraîche (or sour cream)

1 tablespoon caviar or Awesome Olive Spread

WHAT YOU DO

1. Shell and cut the lobster tail into large medallions. Sauté in 1½ teaspoons butter over high heat, for 3 to 5 minutes, or until the flesh is firm and white to the center.

2. Blend lobster on high for two 2-second bursts, or until it is shredded. Set aside.

3. Combine eggs and half-and-half in blender. Blend on low for 3 to 5 seconds, just until blended.

4. Heat a 10-inch nonstick omelet pan over moderate heat for 2 minutes.

5. Put remaining butter into the pan and, when frothy, pour egg mix into pan. Rotate pan for even distribution of eggs.

6. Cook for 1 to 2 minutes, or until eggs begin to set. Push back edges to let uncooked egg run around. When the bottom is set—you can slide a spatula under it—and the top is still slightly liquid, spread the lobster and then the cheese in a line across the center of the omelet.

7. Fold a third of the omelet over toward the middle, and then fold the other outer third into the middle. Cook for about 30 seconds more. Slide onto plate, and top with crème fraîche and a sprinkling of caviar (or Awesome Olive Spread, page 37).

MAKES 2 SERVINGS

THE PERFECT SERVE: You can make 1 large omelet and cut it in half, or divide the egg mix in two, and make 2 smaller omelets. Cut thin wedges of lemon and tuck them alongside the omelet. Garnish with a sprig of parsley.

Date Food

Bullwinkle's Chocolate Mousse

IF ONLY YOU WERE A MASTER composer, you could write her an opera. Instead, compose an aria for her tastebuds with this classic and classy dessert—every note perfection. As final touches go, none can match chocolate mousse for a perfect way to end a meal.

WHAT YOU NEED

1 12-ounce package semisweet chocolate chips

3 large organic eggs

2 cups heavy cream

1 teaspoon granulated sugar

½ teaspoon orange zest

WHAT YOU DO

1. Combine chocolate chips and eggs in blender.

2. Mix heavy cream and sugar in pan over medium heat, stirring until hot but not boiling (about 2 minutes).

3. Pour cream slowly over chocolate as you blend on low. Add orange zest and blend until mix is smooth (no white streaks), about 1 minute.

4. Pour into individual glasses, bowls, or ramekins in which you'll serve the mousse. Chill covered for at least 4 hours before serving. The mousse will keep for several days.

MAKES 4 TO 6 SERVINGS

OUTSTANDING OPTIONS: There are a lot of different ways to customize this dessert, depending on your taste (or hers). To make it denser along the lines of a rich pudding, eliminate the eggs. In any case, fresh organic eggs are best for using raw. To add some zip to the mix, replace half the cream with 1 cup Bailey's Irish Cream, or put a shot of brandy in with the chocolate before adding the hot cream.

THE PERFECT SERVE: If you're counting on this dessert to truly capture a heart and all that comes with it, a little more effort is called for. Go to a gourmet shop and buy a disposable pastry bag and tip, and preformed chocolate boats (or other preformed chocolate container). Chill the mousse in a bowl, and when ready to serve, scoop it into the pastry bag and pipe into the chocolate containers. Shave a little white chocolate over the top and *voilà*, a masterpiece.

GOOD GUY ADVICE: You should never serve food containing raw egg to pregnant women, infants, the elderly, or anyone with a compromised immune system. If you are concerned about the quality of the eggs you buy (salmonella in eggs comes from the chickens being kept in unsanitary conditions), make the denser version of this dessert by leaving the eggs out.

Melon-y's Granita

ICE ON THE TONGUE COOLS THE BODY, BUT A cool tongue, used correctly, inflames the passion. Or at least that's what the *Kama Sutra* says. This much is certainly true: If you want everyone's tongue to be happy share this refreshing frozen treat.

WHAT YOU NEED

2 cups water

¾ cup granulated sugar

1 large ripe cantaloupe or small honeydew melon

¼ cup freshly squeezed lemon juice (about 3 large lemons)

¼ teaspoon orange zest

Dash ground ginger

WHAT YOU DO

1. Combine water and sugar in a medium saucepan. Bring to a boil over medium heat, stirring occasionally. Boil until thick, about 5 minutes. Put aside and let cool.

2. Peel and seed melon and cut into coarse pieces. Blend on medium for 15 seconds, or until smooth. Add lemon juice, orange zest, ginger, and cooled syrup, and blend on medium for 1 minute.

3. Spoon into plastic ice cube trays. Freeze until the mix is firm but not completely solid.

4. Blend the granita cubes on medium for five to seven 2-second bursts, or until finely shredded. Serve immediately, with mint sprig garnish.

MAKES 4 SERVINGS

Satin Sheet Crème Brûlée

EVEN THE STRONGEST WOMAN cannot resist the velvet smoothness of this creamy custard and its hard, caramelized crust. It's like angels dancing on her tongue. Honestly, my friend, if she isn't yours after you serve her this, she never will be.

WHAT YOU NEED

6 egg yolks

2 cups heavy cream

½ cup granulated sugar

2 teaspoons pure vanilla extract

Light brown sugar to cover

WHAT YOU DO

1. Preheat oven to 350°F.

2. Blend egg yolks on low for 5 seconds.

3. Heat cream and sugar over medium heat, stirring constantly. Remove when the cream is scalding but before it boils. With blender running on low, slowly pour a thin stream of the cream mix over the eggs in the blender.

4. Leave the blender running and add the vanilla. Blend for 5 seconds more.

5. Pour through cheesecloth or strainer, into individual ramekins. Place ramekins in baking pan, and fill pan with warm water halfway up the ramekins.

6. Bake for 25 to 30 minutes, or just until the tops of the brûlée begin to brown. Remove and let cool. After 10 minutes, put the ramekins into the refrigerator.

7. Chill for at least 2 hours before serving. To serve, cover the top of the brûlée with a thin layer of brown sugar. Place the ramekins on a pan and position 4 inches under broiler. Broil about 3 minutes, or until the sugar has caramelized into a crust.

MAKES 6 SERVINGS

SHOP TIP. Pure vanilla extract has a much richer taste, and a much higher price tag, than imitation vanilla extract. The difference is noticeable in a recipe like this where the vanilla plays a strong role. Don't make a great dessert mediocre; buy the real thing.

CHAPTER 4

Mom's Best

Dear old Mom. Where would you be without her? She washed laundry a doctor wouldn't touch, took care of you when you were sick, and, most of all, she did all the cooking. All of it. The way she did it, it was more than cooking—she matched meal to mood, food to occasion, making memories in the process. Mom rocked.

Mom was no gourmet; the secret to her cooking was the big dose of soul she added to every dish. She just made simple food that made you feel happy. And the funny thing is, that same food can still make you feel happy. You big sap you.

God bless her, she never worried about cholesterol, or fat, or carbs, or free radicals. She focused on that old-fashioned notion of flavor and comfort. You remember flavor, don't you? That's where you ate something and your tongue got all joyful. It's still there, flavor, just waiting to be rediscovered.

So put on your old baseball cap, grab your appetite, and get that blender ready for traveling, junior. Cause we're headed on one bodaciously tasty trip down memory lane, courtesy of the greatest woman in your life—Mom.

Fundamental French Toast

MOM COULD TEACH AN OBJECT lesson in turning plain, ordinary white bread into a breakfast treat worthy of birthdays, snow days, and other special events. Any morning with her French Toast was a morning well started. Now you can re-create Mom's magic (sans the kiss on the cheek).

WHAT YOU NEED

4 large eggs

½ teaspoon cinnamon

¼ teaspoon ground ginger

¼ teaspoon salt

¼ teaspoon pure vanilla extract

¼ cup half-and-half

4 tablespoons salted butter

6 to 8 thick slices bread

1 tablespoon confectioners sugar

WHAT YOU DO

1. Preheat oven to 250°F.

2. Combine eggs, spices, vanilla, and half-and-half in blender. Blend on high for 15 to 20 seconds, or until well mixed. Empty into a bowl. Or you can soak the bread in the blender, like I do. It's easy and one less bowl to wash.

3. Heat a tablespoon of butter on a griddle or in a large skillet.

4. Dip a slice of bread into the egg mix until soaked. Be careful that it doesn't pull apart. Cook in skillet over medium heat for 3 to 5 minutes on each side, or until dark brown.

5. Repeat with the rest of the bread, adding butter as needed to keep the pieces from sticking. Keep cooked toast warm in oven while you finish cooking all the bread.

6. Sprinkle toast with confectioners' sugar before serving. Serve with real maple syrup.

MAKES 6 TO 8 PIECES OF FRENCH TOAST

THE PERFECT SERVE: Heat the syrup before serving the toast. The warm syrup doesn't cool the toast and heating it brings out the flavor.

Mom's Best

Saturday-Morning Pancakes

FESS UP. EVERY ONCE IN A while, when you have nothing to do on a Saturday morning, you get up late, turn on the cartoons, and regress. But no visit back to your childhood is complete without the simple pleasure of a tall stack of flapjacks.

WHAT YOU NEED

1 cup all-purpose flour

2 tablespoons granulated sugar

1 teaspoon baking powder

½ teaspoon baking soda

¼ teaspoon salt

Dash cinnamon

2 tablespoons canola oil

1 cup plain yogurt

¼ teaspoon pure vanilla extract

1 large egg

WHAT YOU DO

1. Combine all dry ingredients in blender. Blend on low for 2 minutes, or until thoroughly combined. Set aside.

2. Combine oil, yogurt, vanilla, and egg in blender and blend on medium for 15 seconds.

3. Slowly add dry mix to blended liquid, with blender running on low. Blend until all major lumps are gone, about 20 to 30 seconds.

4. Heat griddle or large skillet over medium heat, until cold water flicked onto the surface bounces and sizzles.

5. Pour saucer-sized circles of batter for each pancake, flipping when air bubbles rise to the surface and pop. Cook until dark golden brown on both sides, about 3 minutes per side.

MAKES 6 TO 8 MEDIUM PANCAKES

GOOD GUY ADVICE: Mom never made you clean up, but did you notice you don't live with Mom anymore? Luckily for you, the blender is as easy to clean as it is to cook with. After blending, fill the canister with the hottest water your tap can produce. Add a couple squirts of dishwashing liquid and run the blender on high with the top on. Empty it and do the same with two loads of very hot water. Then place the canister upside down on a dish towel to dry.

Awful (Good) Waffles

IHOP, SCHMIHOP. YEAH, IF YOU WEREN'T your mom's son, you might pile in the car and drive downtown to pay eight bucks for a couple of waffles. But Mom taught you right. You make your waffles at home, with a little cornmeal to mellow the sweetness and add some crunch.

WHAT YOU NEED

½ teaspoon flaxseed

¾ cup all-purpose flour

3 tablespoons yellow cornmeal

Dash cinnamon

2 teaspoons baking powder

2½ teaspoons granulated sugar

¼ teaspoon salt

1 large egg

¾ cup half-and-half

¼ cup canola oil

WHAT YOU DO

1. Preheat your waffle maker or waffle griddle. Preheat oven to 250°F if you'll need to keep waffles warm between batches.

2. Blend flaxseed on medium for three 2-second bursts. Add the other dry ingredients to blender, and blend on medium for 2 minutes. Set aside.

3. Place all liquid ingredients in a blender and blend on medium for 10 seconds.

4. With blender running on low, add dry ingredients at a slow and steady pace. Blend just until combined, not entirely smooth.

5. Pour batter over waffle grids and bake about 5 minutes, or until steam no longer escapes.

6. Remove and serve with pats of unsalted butter and your favorite syrup.

MAKES 6 LARGE WAFFLES

THE PERFECT SERVE: These waffles have a heartier flavor than sweet Belgian-style waffles, making them excellent partners for sweet fruit such as blueberries or strawberries.

GOOD GUY ADVICE: Don't spend time halving this recipe just because you're only making waffles for you. Make the full complement of waffles and freeze what you don't eat. They hold up well to reheating and beat that bowl of Frosty-Os you were planning on having Monday morning.

Simply Satisfying Scramble

EVERY SO OFTEN YOU WANT EGGS, but you don't want to fuss with folding over an omelet or making sure the yolks don't break in your fried eggs. Sometimes the uncomplicated way really is the best. So break a couple shells, cook some bacon, push a button, and let the satisfaction begin.

WHAT YOU NEED

4 large eggs

½ cup grated Swiss cheese

1 tablespoon half-and-half

4 strips bacon, cooked until crisp

3 tablespoon butter

WHAT YOU DO

1. Combine eggs, cheese, and half-and-half in blender and blend on low for 10 seconds. Crumble bacon into blender and blend on low for 2 seconds.

2. Heat butter in skillet until frothy. Add egg mix, and fold over sections as they cook. When done, eggs should still be moist, but not wet.

MAKES 2 SERVINGS

OUTSTANDING OPTIONS: For that real comfort food taste, cook the eggs in the same skillet as the bacon, using the leftover bacon fat in place of the butter.

Green with Envy Pea Soup

A VISIT FROM AUNT SELMA ALWAYS meant Mom got a break from kitchen duties and the rest of the family got treated to Selma's finest recipe—the best use of peas since cafeteria food fights.

WHAT YOU NEED

1 small yellow onion

3 cups chicken broth

1 tablespoon all-purpose flour

2 tablespoons salted butter

1 10-ounce package frozen green peas

¼ teaspoon dried mustard

¼ teaspoon cumin

1 cup half-and-half

Salt and pepper to taste

3 strips bacon, cooked until crisp

WHAT YOU DO

1. Peel and quarter onion. Blend on high for two 2-second bursts.

2. Add 1 cup broth, flour, butter, and peas to blender. Blend on medium for 20 to 30 seconds, or until smooth.

3. Empty mix into saucepan over high heat. Add mustard and cumin and let simmer for 2 to 3 minutes. Add remaining broth. Cover and bring to boil.

4. Reduce to simmer for 5 minutes. Stir in half-and-half and add salt and pepper to taste.

5. Serve with crumbled bacon over top.

MAKES 4 SERVINGS

OUTSTANDING OPTIONS: Add a little zip to this soup by frying up some ham chunks in the saucepan before you heat the soup. Mix in the ham drippings, and add the ham right before serving.

Creamy Dijon Dressing

MOM KNEW FANCY. SHE COULD WHIP out that dress that got Dad's motor running, slip on some heels, smack on a coat of lipstick, and make a special occasion out of any meal. And fancy meant dressing the salad up, too. Follow Mom's lead for your own fancy affair.

WHAT YOU NEED

1 large clove garlic

1 teaspoon chopped fresh chives (about 5 chives)

¼ cup buttermilk

3 tablespoons mayonnaise

1 tablespoon olive oil

1 tablespoon Dijon mustard

Dash Tabasco

WHAT YOU DO

1. Peel and quarter garlic and combine in blender with chives and buttermilk. Blend on high for 5 to 7 seconds.

2. Add the rest of the ingredients and blend on medium for 30 seconds.

3. Serve immediately or keep in refrigerator in a covered container until use.

MAKES DRESSING FOR 4 LARGE SALADS

Mom's Fantastic French Dressing

FRENCH DRESSING IS just like your favorite football jersey—not right for a fancy dinner party, but perfect in less formal circumstances. There's just no better way to bring some flavor to a hunk of distinctly unfancy iceberg lettuce.

WHAT YOU NEED

⅔ cup canola oil

½ cup ketchup

1 tablespoon mayonnaise

2 tablespoons red wine vinegar

1 tablespoon sugar

1 teaspoon paprika

½ teaspoon dried mustard

Dash cayenne

WHAT YOU DO

1. Combine all ingredients in blender, in order listed.

2. Blend on high for 2 minutes, or until consistency is completely smooth and dressing is a uniform color.

MAKES ENOUGH FOR 6 LARGE SALADS

Mom's Best

Home on the Range Ranch Dressing

RANCHES, WHO needs them? Rattlesnakes, roosters waking you up, that lovely smell of cow patties everywhere. No wonder cowboys are a dying breed. You can get all the ranch experience you need with this tangy dressing.

WHAT YOU NEED

1 small garlic clove

2 teaspoons fresh parsley (about 8 sprigs)

1 cup mayonnaise

1 cup buttermilk

2 scallions, trimmed

¼ teaspoon paprika

Dash cayenne

¼ teaspoon salt

¼ teaspoon fresh-ground black pepper

WHAT YOU DO

1. Peel garlic and cut stems off parsley. Combine in blender and blend on high for 3 seconds.

2. Add the rest of the ingredients and blend on high for 10 seconds.

3. Use immediately or chill.

MAKES ENOUGH DRESSING FOR 8 SALADS

A MAN'S WHIRLED

Green God Dressing

IT PUZZLED YOUR PARENTS, YOUR LOVE OF a salad dressing the color of the Hulk's skin. You were a strange kid and that was just one more thing that proved it, but Mom bought you the dressing anyway. How things have changed. Now you're a strange adult, and you can make your own weird-colored dressing.

WHAT YOU NEED

3 scallions (tops only)

1 teaspoon chives

12 sprigs parsley

1 cup mayonnaise

¾ cup sour cream

1 tablespoon lemon juice

½ teaspoon salt

2 teaspoons white vinegar

WHAT YOU DO

1. Blend scallion tops, chives, and parsley on high for 3 seconds.

2. Add mayonnaise and sour cream and blend on low for 30 seconds.

3. Add remaining ingredients and blend on medium for 1 minute.

4. Chill for 1 hour before serving.

MAKES ENOUGH DRESSING FOR 8 SALADS

Mom's Best

Mambo Italiano Dressing

REMEMBER WHEN YOU USED TO GO to restaurants with your parents and they'd order you a salad with "Italian" dressing? You never knew what you were going to get. But now you're in the driver's seat, so make sure your salad is covered by the original, the authentic, the real Italian.

WHAT YOU NEED

2 small cloves garlic

6 tablespoons olive oil

2 sprigs fresh parsley

2 tablespoons red wine vinegar

1 tablespoon fresh-squeezed lemon juice

1 teaspoon dried basil

Pinch dried oregano

WHAT YOU DO

1. Peel and chop the garlic into coarse pieces. Combine in blender with olive oil and blend on high for three 2-second bursts, or until finely chopped.

2. Add parsley and blend on high for two 2-second bursts.

3. Add remaining ingredients and blend on low for 15 to 20 seconds, or until well mixed. Cover and refrigerate until serving.

MAKES DRESSING FOR 4 SALADS

THE PERFECT SERVE: Add salt and pepper to the salad rather than the dressing, to better control the taste.

A MAN'S WHIRLED

Memorable Meat Loaf

THE GODS MAY NOT HAVE GIVEN US the easy life, but they made up for it by giving us the smell of a fresh-cooked meat loaf coming out of the oven. Close your eyes, take a whiff, and it's like sitting down to one of those family feasts that leave everyone in a food stupor. Meat loaf. Thank the gods.

WHAT YOU NEED

Meat Loaf

1 medium yellow onion

2 cloves garlic

2 tablespoons canola oil

1 stalk celery

1½ teaspoons salt

½ teaspoon fresh-ground black pepper

½ teaspoon hot sauce

1 large egg

½ cup tomato sauce

¾ cup bread crumbs

¼ cup half-and-half

2 pounds lean ground beef

Glaze

1 tablespoon light brown sugar

1 tablespoon cider vinegar

¼ teaspoon salt

¼ teaspoon cinnamon

¾ cup tomato sauce

WHAT YOU DO

1. Preheat oven to 350°F.

2. Peel and coarsely chop onion and garlic. Combine in blender with oil, and blend on high for 3 seconds.

3. Chop celery and combine with salt and pepper, hot sauce, egg, and tomato sauce in blender. Blend on medium for 10 seconds.

4. With blender running, add bread crumbs and half-and-half. Blend on medium for an additional 15 seconds, or until thoroughly mixed. Scrape down sides as necessary.

5. Place meat in large mixing bowl and pour blender mix over it. Combine by kneading, until thoroughly mixed. Form into a loaf using 9-by-5 nonstick pan as mold.

6. Remove loaf from pan onto nonstick baking sheet.

7. Blend glaze ingredients for 20 seconds on medium, and pour over top of meat loaf. Bake for 1 hour, 15 minutes.

MAKES 8 SERVINGS

OUTSTANDING OPTIONS: This is an extremely moist meat loaf. If you prefer a drier version, cook the meat loaf in the loaf pan, and bake for an additional 15 minutes.

Mom's Best

Uncle Gino's Chicken Cacciatore

YOU CAN TAKE UNCLE GINO out of the old country, but you can't take the old country out of Uncle Gino. To prove it, here's his favorite dish—Sicily's most famous export next to Sambuca and Uncle Gino himself.

WHAT YOU NEED

2 large chicken breasts, bone in (about 2 pounds)

½ cup olive oil

1 teaspoon salt

1 teaspoon pepper

6 cloves garlic

1 medium yellow onion

1 small green bell pepper

1 small red bell pepper

1 stalk celery

1 teaspoon oregano

1 teaspoon thyme

¼ cup Marsala

1 28-ounce can diced tomatoes

WHAT YOU DO

1. Preheat oven to 350°F.

2. Saturate the breasts with ¼ cup olive oil. Sprinkle with salt and fresh-ground pepper, and rub into the breasts. Put the breasts in a baking pan, and bake for 45 minutes.

3. Peel garlic and onion. Chop coarsely and combine in blender with remaining olive oil. Blend on medium for five 3-second bursts, or until well chopped. Empty blender into large saucepan.

4. Seed bell peppers and cut off ends of celery stalk. Chop into coarse pieces. Blend each color pepper and celery on their own. Blend for two to three 2-second bursts, or until the vegetables are coarsely chopped.

5. Put baked chicken breasts into saucepan and cook on high. Sauté for 5 minutes, or until garlic begins to brown. Add vegetables and oregano and thyme.

6. Add Marsala and bring to a boil. Reduce to simmer and add tomatoes.

7. Simmer for 1½ to 2 hours, adding water if sauce becomes too thick. Turn chicken after 45 minutes. Serve with small side of spaghetti covered with some of the cacciatore sauce.

MAKES 2 FULL-MEAL SERVINGS

GOOD GUY ADVICE: If you have to blend a lot of vegetables to a coarse consistency, take this shortcut. Put the vegetables in the blender canister and fill to just above their level with cold water. Blend as necessary to chop the vegetables, then drain the water.

Down Home Dumplings with Red-Eye Gravy

IF YOU'RE LUCKY ENOUGH TO HAVE A mama with roots in the Deep South, then you've tasted this rib-sticking dinner straight off a roadhouse menu. The filling dumplings temper a gravy that'll keep you up all night. The Appalachians call it "Clouds in Mud." You'll just call it delicious.

WHAT YOU NEED

Dumplings

1½ cups all-purpose flour

1½ teaspoons baking powder

½ teaspoon salt

¾ cup whole milk

1 large egg

1 tablespoon salted butter, softened

½ teaspoon fresh-ground black pepper

Gravy

2 tablespoons salted butter

1 tablespoon dark brown sugar

Leavings from a skillet of bacon

2 cups strong black coffee

1 cup water

2 tablespoons flour

WHAT YOU DO

Gravy

1. Combine butter and sugar with hot bacon leavings in their skillet. Stir in coffee and water over medium heat.

2. Stir in flour and reduce. Stir often as gravy reduces.

Dumplings

1. Combine flour, baking powder, and salt in blender. Blend on low for 2 minutes. Set aside.

2. Combine milk, egg, and butter in blender. Blend on high for 10 seconds. Add powdered mix and black pepper, and blend on low for 1 minute, or until completely combined.

3. Drop mix into simmering gravy one small dumpling at a time (about a teaspoonful). Cook for 3 minutes on each side or until puffy, and remove. Pour gravy over top and serve.

MAKES 4 SERVINGS

OUTSTANDING OPTIONS: Red-Eye Gravy is an acquired taste that will put hair on your chest. If it's a little too rough for your palate, substitute packaged gravy mix.

Mom's Best

Garlic Smashed Potatoes

WHERE WOULD THOSE TRADITIONAL Sunday dinners have been without a big bowl of mashed potatoes? That hearty staple just seems to go perfectly with everything else on the plate. This version adds some zip because, well, let's face it, Mom wasn't exactly adventurous in the kitchen.

WHAT YOU NEED

2 large Idaho potatoes

4 cloves peeled garlic

6 tablespoons salted butter

1 cup whole milk

1 tablespoon heavy cream

½ teaspoon salt

½ teaspoon pepper

WHAT YOU DO

1. Scrub the potatoes and cut them into quarters. Put them in a pot and cover with cold water. Bring water to a boil. Boil for 20 minutes, or until potatoes are tender (test with a fork).

2. Blend garlic with ¼ cup water on high for 3 to 7 seconds, or until finely minced. Heat minced garlic in pan over low heat.

3. Wait until water evaporates, and add butter. Melt butter and garlic on low heat and simmer for 5 minutes.

4. Remove potatoes and peel (or leave skins on for more variety and texture in the dish).

5. Combine half of the potatoes, butter-garlic mix, cream, and milk in blender. Blend on low for five to seven 2-second bursts. Scrape sides down as necessary.

6. Set aside in bowl and blend second half of ingredients as before. When finished, combine with potatoes in bowl, stirring in salt and pepper as you combine the halves. Serve hot.

MAKES 4 SERVINGS

THE PERFECT SERVE: These potatoes are wonderful as is, but add some chopped chives for a nice finishing touch. You can also make packaged gravy mix for a more traditional approach to the dish.

Johnny Crack Corn Pudding

WHO CAN SAY WHAT GENIUS thought up making a bread pudding with corn? Maybe Mom came up with this one all by herself. Maybe it was crazy Aunt Sheila. Maybe it's the demented masterpiece of the Corngrowers of America. Whoever it was, they certainly knew an indispensable Sunday dinner side dish when they saw one.

WHAT YOU NEED

1 small yellow onion

1 small clove peeled garlic

¼ cup stuffed green olives

1 15-ounce can whole kernel corn

3 large eggs

1½ cups half-and-half

1 teaspoon granulated sugar

¼ teaspoon paprika

Dash cayenne

¼ teaspoon dry mustard

Salt and pepper to taste

1 cup bread crumbs

WHAT YOU DO

1. Preheat oven to 375°F.

2. Peel onion and chop into coarse pieces. Blend on high for 3 seconds.

3. Add all other ingredients except bread crumbs. Blend on medium for 5 seconds, or just until mixed.

4. Add bread crumbs and blend on medium for 10 seconds, or until crumbs are thoroughly mixed in. Scrape down sides as necessary.

5. Pour into greased 2-quart casserole dish. Bake for 50 minutes, or until the pudding doesn't jiggle and the top is golden brown.

6. Remove and let cool for 10 minutes before serving.

MAKES 4 TO 6 SERVINGS AS A SIDE DISH

Mom's Best

THE PERFECT SERVE: You can make individual servings of corn pudding by baking in separate crockery soup bowls. That way everybody knows from the start how much they're going to get, and they won't go trying to take more than their share. No need to mention names. The guilty parties know who they are.

Family Picnic Egg Salad

LET'S FACE IT, MOST EGG SALADS ARE to flavor what paintings on velvet are to modern art. The three words that best describe them are bland, bland, and bland. But this version redefines the genre, making it a major player at any reunion, family or otherwise.

WHAT YOU NEED

2 shallots

½ red onion

1 teaspoon fresh tarragon

¼ cup mayonnaise

¼ teaspoon salt

¼ teaspoon fresh-ground pepper

1 teaspoon white vinegar

1 tablespoon Dijon mustard

4 extra-large hard-boiled eggs

WHAT YOU DO

1. Peel and quarter shallots and onion. Combine with tarragon leaves in blender, and blend on high for three 2-second bursts, or until finely chopped.

2. Add the rest of the ingredients except for the eggs and blend on medium for 5 seconds. Scrape down the sides and blend for 5 seconds more.

3. Shell and quarter the eggs. Add to blender and blend on medium for three 2-second bursts, or until eggs are chopped well.

4. Empty blender into bowl, and mix with fork to ensure blending. Serve at once or refrigerate covered until use.

MAKES 4 SMALL SERVINGS

THE PERFECT SERVE: This egg salad can be a solo player heaped on a bed of lettuce leaves, or can be part of a bread ensemble, making one of the best egg salad sandwiches you've ever tasted.

GOOD GUY ADVICE: A page from the book of basics: "Hard-Boiling an Egg 101." Put eggs in a pot with enough water to cover them. Heat the pot on high. Once the water starts boiling, let it boil for 10 minutes and remove the pot from the heat. Let the pot sit for 5 more minutes, and then run cold water over the eggs. Presto, perfectly boiled eggs.

All-Season Applesauce

IF JOHNNY APPLESEED COULD BUST HIS hump crossing the country on foot so that the rest of us would have enough apples, then it's only decent that we do something with all these apples. And cool, smooth, luscious applesauce seems as fitting a tribute as any.

WHAT YOU NEED

4 large ripe, red apples (McIntosh or Red Delicious), peeled and cored

½ cup cold water

Dash lemon juice

½ teaspoon cinnamon

3 tablespoons honey

WHAT YOU DO

1. Quarter apples. Combine half portions of all ingredients in blender.

2. Blend on high for 5 to 10 seconds, until apples are broken down. Then blend on low for 15 to 20 seconds until smooth. Repeat with other half of ingredients.

3. Mix two halves, and serve immediately, or chill for serving later.

MAKES 4 SERVINGS AS A SIDE DISH

Mom's Best

Shores of Sicily Marinara

IF YOUR IDEA OF SPAGHETTI SAUCE comes from Chef Boyardee, it's high time you got back to Mom's basics—fresh ingredients cooked a good long time. This rich sauce uses the bounty of the garden to create an Italian classic that ranks right up there with Sophia Loren and the Tower of Pisa.

WHAT YOU NEED

4 cloves garlic

2 anchovy fillets

3 tablespoons olive oil

2 medium yellow onions

2 stalks celery

1 teaspoon oregano

½ teaspoon rosemary

1 teaspoon salt

Large dash fresh-ground black pepper

¼ cup fresh parsley

1 small green bell pepper

3 fresh basil leaves

½ cup Marsala

2 28-ounce cans crushed tomatoes

1 6-ounce can tomato paste

1 teaspoon granulated sugar

WHAT YOU DO

1. Combine garlic, anchovies, and olive oil in blender. Blend on high for 3 to 5 seconds. Empty into large pot, over medium heat.

2. Peel onions and chop onions and celery into coarse pieces. Combine in blender and blend for three 2-second bursts on medium, or until well chopped. Add to pot.

3. Combine oregano, rosemary, salt, and pepper in blender, and blend on high for 3 seconds. When onions are soft and clear, add spice mix to pot and stir.

4. Cut stems off parsley and chop bell pepper into coarse pieces. Combine with basil in blender. Blend on medium for 2 to 4 seconds, or until finely chopped. Add to pot. Add Marsala and bring to boil.

5. Add tomatoes, paste, and sugar. Stir well and reduce to simmer. Simmer for 3 hours, adding water periodically to prevent ingredients from sticking to pan.

MAKES 4 SERVINGS

THE PERFECT SERVE: Serve this sauce with spaghetti cooked *al dente* (literally, "to the tooth," meaning the pasta still has some resistance when you bite it). You shouldn't need the Sopranos to teach you that anything but freshly grated Parmesan is a crime against the old country.

Popover Clouds

POPOVERS ARE THE CHARACTER ACTORS OF THE dinner table. Need something to sop up that chili in the bottom of the bowl? Popovers are your sauce sponge. Smother them with butter and they're better than biscuits. Put a little jam on them, and they show up croissants.

WHAT YOU NEED

2 large eggs

1 cup whole milk

¾ cup all-purpose flour

¼ teaspoon salt

WHAT YOU DO

1. Preheat oven to 425°F.

2. Combine ingredients in the blender. Blend on low for 5 seconds, and then on medium for 15 seconds.

3. Grease muffin tins. Pour batter into tins, filling each cavity halfway. Bake 25 to 35 minutes, or until puffed and brown.

MAKES 12 TO 14 POPOVERS

Heavenly Hot Chocolate

YOU DON'T NEED A HALO AND HARP TO enjoy a chocolaty favorite that is truly out of this world. The rich, spicy taste makes a bitter-cold earthbound day something to celebrate. And (ironically), it's sinfully delicious.

WHAT YOU NEED

½ cup semisweet chocolate chips

½ teaspoon orange zest

2 cups whole milk

¼ teaspoon ground nutmeg

Dash cinnamon

WHAT YOU DO

1. Combine chocolate chips and orange zest in blender.

2. Heat milk until scalding, but not boiling. Pour into blender, with blender on medium. Blend on medium for 30 seconds.

3. Add nutmeg and cinnamon, and blend on medium for 5 seconds. Serve hot.

MAKES 2 BIG MUGS

Nana's Pumpkin Pie

GROWING UP, THERE WERE BASICALLY TWO reasons to love Thanksgiving: the thrill of sneaking a hit off your dad's Seven-and-Seven, and the long-awaited taste of your grandma's pumpkin pie. These days, you can make your own Seven-and-Seven (although why you would want to is a mystery), and now you can bring back Grandma's classic—at any time of the year.

WHAT YOU NEED

¾ cup granulated sugar

½ teaspoon salt

1 teaspoon cinnamon

½ teaspoon ground ginger

¼ teaspoon ground cloves

Dash nutmeg

¼ teaspoon allspice

2 large eggs

1 15-ounce can pumpkin

1 12-ounce can evaporated milk

1 9-inch deep-dish pie shell, unbaked

WHAT YOU DO

1. Preheat oven to 425°F.

2. Combine sugar and spices in blender. Blend on medium for 2 minutes. Set aside.

3. Put eggs in blender and blend on medium for 3 seconds. Add pumpkin and blend on medium for 10 seconds, or just until mixed.

4. Slowly add sugar mix and blend on low for 15 to 20 seconds, or until ingredients are combined. Scrape down sides and stir as necessary.

5. Slowly add evaporated milk while blending on low. Blend for 10 to 15 seconds, or just until milk is mixed in. Scrape down and stir as necessary.

6. Pour mix into pie shell. Bake for 15 minutes, then lower temperature to 350°F and bake for an additional 45 to 55 minutes, or until knife inserted in center of pie comes out clean.

7. Remove from oven and let cool on a wire rack for at least 15 minutes before serving.

MAKES 6 TO 8 SERVINGS

THE PERFECT SERVE: Pumpkin Pie's best friend is Homespun Cream (page 137). Don't make them spend dessert time apart.

GOOD GUY ADVICE: Many baked goods should be cooled on a wire rack right after they come out of the oven, to allow air to circulate around the bottom, evenly dissipating the heat. But who has a wire rack lying around? If you have a gas stove, remove one off the burner rings and sit it on the counter as a cooling rack. Otherwise, remove the entire rack from the oven and place it on a large flat surface for cooling.

Very Berry Mousse

MOM KNEW EVERYTHING. SHE KNEW HOW to fix any household appliance with pantyhose and a twist tie. She knew where you hid your *Playboy*s and your cigarettes. She knew when the old man needed the carrot and when he needed the stick. And Mom knew how to make a 5-minute dessert that proved gelatin was for suckers. Learn from Mom.

WHAT YOU NEED

2 8-ounce packages cream cheese, extremely soft

¾ cup frozen, unsweetened whole strawberries, thawed (about 8 strawberries)

⅔ cup frozen raspberries, thawed

1 teaspoon lemon juice

½ cup confectioners' sugar

½ cup heavy cream

WHAT YOU DO

1. Cut cream cheese into cubes. Combine thawed berries, cream cheese, lemon juice, and powdered sugar in blender, and blend on medium for 20 to 30 seconds, or until smooth. Stop and scrape down sides as necessary. Set aside.

2. Whip heavy cream in blender on high for 5 to 7 seconds, or until stiff.

3. Add berry mix in a steady stream, blending on medium. Blend for 30 seconds total.

4. Spoon mousse into dessert dishes. Chill covered for 4 hours or overnight.

MAKES 6 SERVINGS

Mom's Best

Banana Nut Bread

YOUR GREEN LANTERN LUNCH BOX. PHONES with dials. Evel Knievel and the Reggie candy bar. And Banana Nut Bread. If the smell of Banana Nut Bread baking doesn't take you back to a soft-lens, sepia-toned, Norman Rockwell version of yesteryear, then you, sir, are a soulless lout.

WHAT YOU NEED

2½ cups all-purpose flour

3 teaspoons baking powder

¼ teaspoon cinnamon

½ teaspoon salt

¾ cup pecans

3 medium overripe bananas

⅓ cup unsalted butter, softened

1 large egg

½ cup whole milk

¼ cup heavy cream

½ teaspoon vanilla

1 cup granulated sugar

WHAT YOU DO

1. Preheat oven to 350°F.

2. Blend flour, baking powder, cinnamon, and salt on medium for 2 minutes. Set aside in large bowl.

3. Blend pecans on medium for five to seven 3-second bursts, or until finely chopped, or blend to desired texture. Add to flour mix.

4. Break bananas in pieces and combine in blender with butter, egg, milk, cream, vanilla, and sugar in that order. Blend on medium for 1 minute.

5. Empty blender into dry ingredients and mix with a large fork until thoroughly combined.

6. Pour batter into greased 9-by-5 loaf pan. Bake for 1 hour. Remove and let cool on a wire rack for 10 minutes, then remove the bread from the pan and serve.

MAKES 6 TO 8 SERVINGS

THE PERFECT SERVE: Subtle as it is, banana nut bread serves as the perfect foil for a heaping scoop of vanilla ice cream. Make it even more decadent with a dollop of Holy Hot Fudge Topping (page 131).

CHAPTER 5

Party Favors

"The man with a blender is a man ever ready to party." Caligula said that over two thousand years ago, and it remains true today. Where there's a blender, there's a party just waiting to happen. The blender was the party instrument of choice in ancient Rome, and was actually to blame for the downfall of the Roman Empire. That, and public displays of immorality, which frankly went hand in hand with the use of the blender.

All of which is a good argument for the responsible use of the blender, and its alcoholic creations.

Who can say what it is about blenders that just screams "Party!"? Maybe it's those people who, when they see a blender and bottles of booze, scream "Party!" Maybe. But we know for certain, if we know nothing else, that there is something about the sound of a blender running that creates a Pavlovian anticipation of wonderful, intoxicating concoctions. More than can be said for the sound of a beer being popped open.

Associations with partying are just more evidence that blenders really can be fun. More fun than the proverbial barrel of monkeys. Blenders are fun because they make frozen drinks, which are the liquid fuse to dynamite parties. Yes, it's all fun till someone puts an eye out. Which hopefully will never happen if you're using your blender correctly.

So put on your safety eyewear and start your machine. It's officially time to get the party started.

> **Interesting note that you know you should absolutely read and pay attention to because it's in bold: The "shot" mentioned in the recipes below is the universally accepted measure—exactly 1.5 ounces of intoxicant. But for your purposes, you can take the measure to mean "1 part" as long as you maintain relationships between ingredients. Oh, yeah, please note that these recipes are all for single drinks. Go on, note it. To make a pitcher of any of these, multiply by 4. Just do the multiplication before you start mixing the drinks.**

Magnificent Margarita

NOTHING TAKES THE EDGE OFF A STEAMY summer night quite like a good frozen Margarita. If you've come to associate frozen drinks with bad Club Med vacations, it's time to get over it. This simple mix of a few high-quality ingredients makes for an elegant and incredibly refreshing cocktail.

WHAT YOU NEED

3 shots Herradura Añejo tequila (or other premium gold tequila)

1 shot Cointreau

Juice of 1 lime

Lime wedges

½ shot Grand Marnier

WHAT YOU DO

1. Mix first 3 ingredients in the blender, adding ice to just below the level of the liquid.

2. Blend on medium for 20 seconds, or until all the ice is thoroughly crushed and the drink is entirely blended.

3. Wipe a lime wedge around the rim of a flat Margarita "coupe," and twist the glass upside down in a bed of sea salt to salt the rim (or leave unsalted if the drinker prefers). Pour the blended mix to fill the glass. Make a dent in the peak, and pour in a thimbleful of Grand Marnier. Garnish with a wedge of lime.

WARNING: This is one of the most powerful frozen drinks you're going to come across, and one is the maximum for any but the heartiest souls. For a casual cool cocktail with a bit less power, split this between 2 people or halve the recipe.

SHOP TIP: When you're pricing tequilas, keep in mind the cheaper the tequila, the worse the hangover. And if it has a worm in it, remember: You are what you eat.

Icy Grasshopper

MAYBE YOU THINK THESE ANNOYING LITTLE INSECTS don't bite, but suck down a couple of glasses and you'll know differently. Sweet as candy, this drink goes down smooth. Be careful you don't go down with it.

WHAT YOU NEED

½ shot white crème de cacao

½ shot crème de menthe

1 large scoop vanilla ice cream, softened

¼ cup half-and-half

WHAT YOU DO

1. Combine first 3 ingredients in blender and blend on low for 10 seconds.

2. Add half-and-half through top, and blend on low for 15 seconds, or until drink is thoroughly blended and color is even throughout.

3. Serve in chilled martini glasses.

GOOD GUY ADVICE: You can help keep your frozen concoctions as chilly as possible by freezing the blender canister before you blend—but remove the blade first.

Chocolate Monkey

AREN'T MONKEYS FUNNY? THE WAY THEY JUMP around hanging off things, making nonsense noises and scratching themselves. Those darn monkeys just make me laugh. See the video from your last party lately?

WHAT YOU NEED

½ shot banana liqueur

1 shot crème de cacao

1½ scoops chocolate ice cream, softened

½ shot chocolate syrup

¼ cup whole milk

WHAT YOU DO

1. Combine all ingredients in blender. Liquid should come to just below level of ice cream.

2. Blend on low for 1 minute, or until thoroughly mixed.

3. Serve in highball glass and top with a dollop of whipped cream.

Devil's Tail

LUCIFER IS THE ORIGINAL BAD BOY PARTY ANIMAL, AND IF you want to grab his tail, you better be ready for a hot time. A few of these down the hatch and you might just think you're the king of the underworld yourself.

WHAT YOU NEED

½ shot apricot brandy

1 shot light rum

1 shot pepper vodka

½ shot grenadine

1 tablespoon lime juice

WHAT YOU DO

1. Combine ingredients in blender, and add ice to the level of the fluid.

2. Blend on high for 30 seconds, or until thoroughly mixed.

3. Serve in champagne flute garnished with lemon peel.

GOOD GUY ADVICE: Sweet liquors such as rum can leave a sticky residue that will play havoc with the blade mechanism of a blender. Fill the blender canister with hot water between drinks. When you're ready to blend again, empty the canister and fill with cold water before making a drink, to prevent the ice from melting too quickly.

Iced Berkeley

LET NO MAN FORGET THAT BERKELEY IS A COLLEGE TOWN, and as such must uphold the highest in formal academic standards and behavior beyond repute. Not. It's Berkeley. It's California. It's party time. Lose the books, find a toga, and get blending.

WHAT YOU NEED

½ shot brandy

1 shot light rum

1 tablespoon lemon juice

1 tablespoon passion fruit syrup

WHAT YOU DO

1. Combine all ingredients and fill with crushed ice to the level of fluid.

2. Blend on medium for 45 seconds.

3. Serve in a champagne flute.

Party Favors

Snack Time

of candy treat, the world would be a much nicer place. And vending machine companies would be really, really rich. Just be careful the next morning; don't mistake a sugar coma for a hangover.

WHAT YOU NEED

1 shot butterscotch schnapps

½ shot vodka

½ shot coffee liqueur

1 scoop vanilla ice cream, softened

WHAT YOU DO

1. Combine all ingredients in blender.

2. Blend on low for 20 seconds or until smooth.

3. Serve in highball glass with Kit Kat bar as a stir stick.

SHOP TIP: You have better things to spend your money on than name-brand coffee liqueur. Off brands work just fine for frozen drinks.

Peachy Cream

SOME PAIRS WERE JUST MEANT TO BE: FRED AND GINGER, Fred and Wilma, Fred and Ethel, Fred and Lamont, and, of course, Peaches and Cream. Giving that lovely couple a little zing only improves what was already amazing chemistry.

WHAT YOU NEED

1 shot peach schnapps

1 shot lemon vodka

¼ cup heavy cream

4 frozen peach quarters

WHAT YOU DO

1. Combine ingredients in blender. Blend on medium for two 2-second bursts to break up peach quarters.

2. Blend on high for 20 seconds, or until smooth.

3. Serve in martini glass, garnished with a slice of peach.

Arctic Holiday

TARZAN SWUNG INTO THE TREEHOUSE, TIRED FROM the long day of fighting rampaging elephants. And then there was the thing with the crocodile. "Jane," he said. "Tarzan beat." Jane smiled. "'Tarzan need a vacation," she said, as she started the blender.

WHAT YOU NEED

1 shot peach schnapps

2 shots vodka

¼ cup orange juice

⅓ cup peach nectar

Splash lemon juice

1 shot champagne

WHAT YOU DO

1. Combine all ingredients except for champagne in blender. Add ice to level of liquid.

2. Blend on medium for 1 minute.

3. Pour into red wine glasses and top with a float of champagne.

SHOP TIP: The wise man buys a split—half a bottle—of champagne for making blended drinks. Less to go to waste. And, trust me, you can't taste the difference between Cristal and Korbel in a blended drink, so buy the cheapest split you can find.

Jupiter Bar

LEGAL SAYS NOT TO USE THE NAME OF A CERTAIN CANDY conglomerate, so we used the name of another planet. Stupid Legal. Call it what you will, it's still just like drinking candy, only candy with a nice little adults-only buzz. You won't find that in any Halloween bags.

WHAT YOU NEED

1 shot Cointreau

½ shot dark crème de cacao

¼ cup heavy cream

WHAT YOU DO

1. Combine the ingredients in blender with crushed ice to level of fluid.

2. Blend on high for 20 seconds.

3. Serve in sundae glass, with whipped cream and cherry on top.

Anna's Sweetart

YOU KNOW AN ANNA. SHE MIGHT BE CALLED SUZIE, or Barb, or Diane where you're from, but they're all Annas. Anna's the one that taught you that a beautiful smile can hide fangs. Anna should come with a warning label. So should her drink. Because just like Anna, this drink's a little bit sweet, but with a vicious little bite. Ouch.

WHAT YOU NEED

1 shot vodka

2 tablespoons fresh lime juice

½ large ripe banana, sliced and frozen

1 teaspoon honey

WHAT YOU DO

1. Combine ingredients in blender. Blend on medium for two 2-second bursts to break up bananas.

2. Blend on high for 30 seconds, or until smooth.

3. Serve in the funkiest glasses you have. Garnish with a slice of lime.

GOOD GUY ADVICE: Head off hangovers by alternating a glass of water with every blended drink you quaff.

Screamsicle

YOU SCREAM, I SCREAM, WE ALL SCREAM FOR AN ALCOHOL-laced version of the traditional ice-cream truck push-up. A nice hot afternoon blast with a mellow buzz, and you don't even have to chase the truck.

WHAT YOU NEED

¼ can frozen orange juice concentrate

1 shot gin

1 large scoop vanilla ice cream, softened

½ teaspoon pure vanilla extract

WHAT YOU DO

1. Combine ingredients and blend on medium for 20 to 30 seconds, or until smooth.

2. Serve in highball glass with a slice of orange as garnish.

A MAN'S WHIRLED

Snowstorm

CAN'T . . . GO . . . ANY . . . FARTHER. BLINDED . . . BY . . . the . . . snowstorm. Frostbite . . . setting . . . in. Can't . . . think . . . straight. Must stop . . . and . . . try . . . to . . . warm . . . up. Must . . . stop . . . and . . . rest, but . . . so . . . cold. Ah, what the hell, pour me another.

WHAT YOU NEED

2 shots bourbon

2 tablespoons real cranberry juice (not cranberry cocktail)

Splash fresh lemon juice

1 tablespoon granulated sugar

WHAT YOU DO

1. Combine sugar and lemon juice in blender, and blend on medium for 5 seconds.

2. Add other ingredients and ice to level of fluid, and blend on high for 15 to 20 seconds, or until smooth.

3. Serve in highball glass.

SHOP TIP: Don't buy top-shelf bourbons for frozen drinks or cooking. It's a waste of good bourbon and your money. Stick with bargain brands—you'll never know the difference.

Bananarita

AND THEN CHIQUITA SAID TO THE TALL, DARK STRANGER, "We have no Cointreau, tall, dark stranger, but the banana liqueur, it will work just as well." And the tall, dark stranger thought it odd, but he tasted it and loved it and loved her. "Chiquita," he said, "it is fascinating . . . like you."

WHAT YOU NEED

2 shots tequila

1 shot banana liqueur

1 shot lime juice

WHAT YOU DO

1. Combine the ingredients in blender and blend on medium for 5 seconds. Add crushed ice to level of fluid.

2. Blend on high for 30 seconds, or until smooth.

3. Run a slice of banana around the rim of a Margarita glass and dip rim in confectioners' sugar. Serve with slice of banana as garnish.

Ambush

HE HAD HIS MARGARITA NIGHTS AND LIVED TO TELL THE TALE. Daiquiris? They nearly got him for good, but in the end he had their number too. He took them all on and never went down. But what's this? Oh, a sweet little drink, couldn't be any harm in that, right? Poor fool, never saw it coming.

WHAT YOU NEED

¼ cup half-and-half

1 shot coffee liqueur

1 shot cream of coconut

½ shot light rum

½ shot dark crème de cacao

WHAT YOU DO

1. Combine ingredients in blender, and blend on high for 5 seconds.

2. Add ice to level of fluid, and blend on medium for 20 seconds, or until smooth.

3. Serve in tall glass.

SHOP TIP: You can find cream of coconut in the ethnic food aisle at your local supermarket, or at a well-stocked liquor store.

Deadly Daiquiri

IT'S A FROSTY CLASSIC THAT HEMINGWAY THOUGHT was mighty fine. So much so, that he could put away ten in one trip to the bar. That was Hemingway. He went head to head with Gertrude Stein, ran with the bulls, and hunted lions. You better play it a little safer and stay in the single digits.

WHAT YOU NEED

1 shot Bacardi Silver rum

2 tablespoons fresh lime juice

1 teaspoon powdered sugar

WHAT YOU DO

1. Combine ingredients in blender and blend on high for 5 seconds, or until sugar is completely dissolved.

2. Add ice to the level of the fluid, and blend for 30 seconds.

3. Serve in Margarita glass with wedge of lime as garnish.

Uncle Louie's Golden Caddy

ANY DRINK WITH GALLIANO JUST reeks of old, old school. So save this for one of those muggy August days, sitting in the back booth at Enrico's swapping stories with your goombahs. Just keep your little finger away from the glass; that sticky crap ain't good for the pinkie ring.

WHAT YOU NEED

2 shots white crème de cacao

1 shot Galliano

2 tablespoons half-and-half

WHAT YOU DO

1. Combine all the ingredients in the blender and blend on medium for 5 seconds.

2. Add ice to the level of the fluid and blend on high for 30 seconds, or until it is a uniform color throughout.

3. Serve in a champagne coupe.

Piña Colada

FUNNY THAT SUCH A PRETTY NAME SHOULD TRANSLATE to "strained pineapple." Here's a better translation: "Ice-cold sweet intoxicating aphrodisiac for when the sun is beating down, the sand is too hot to walk on, and her micro-bikini is more micro than bikini." Rolls off the tongue, doesn't it?

WHAT YOU NEED

½ cup unsweetened pineapple juice

2 shots gold rum

¼ cup cream of coconut

WHAT YOU DO

1. Combine ingredients in blender, with ice to level of fluid.

2. Blend on high for 30 seconds.

3. Serve in a tall glass with a miniature umbrella or pineapple spear.

OUTSTANDING OPTIONS: Make a Nutty Colada by substituting amaretto for the rum.

The Walking Dead

IT'S ALL ABOUT THE ZOMBIES. YOU FIGHT THEM, and fight them, and fight them. You shotgun them in half and they keep coming. You hack their heads off and they keep coming. They want your brains, so they just keep coming. Well, if you can't beat them, join them. Cheers.

WHAT YOU NEED

1 shot light rum

1 shot passion fruit syrup

1 shot pineapple juice

1 shot orange juice

1 shot dark rum

½ shot apricot brandy

Splash lime juice

1 teaspoon powdered sugar

Float of gold rum

WHAT YOU DO

1. Combine ingredients in blender, except for the gold rum, and blend on high for 5 seconds.

2. Add ice to the level of the fluid, and blend on high for 30 to 40 seconds, or until smoothly blended.

3. Serve in a highball glass with a pineapple spear and a cherry. Make a dent in the top and float a splash of gold rum on top.

GOOD GUY ADVICE: If you can't find passion fruit syrup, buy passion fruit juice (usually in the grocery aisle with the coconut cream), and mix with 1 teaspoon Bartender's Syrup (page 102).

The Iced Matador

TAKES A BULL TO ICE A MATADOR, AND WHEN the matador is good and truly iced, then you know the bull has won. And they give the bull the matador's cap, and perhaps an ear if the bull has iced him especially well. The Moral: In a bar, enjoy your drink, but beware of the bull.

WHAT YOU NEED

1 shot tequila

¼ cup pineapple juice

Splash lime juice

1 teaspoon Bartender's Syrup (see page 102)

WHAT YOU DO

1. Combine ingredients in blender and blend on high for 5 seconds.

2. Add ice to the level of fluid in the blender. Blend on high for 30 seconds, or until well mixed.

Brain Freeze

A BRAIN FREEZE IS A COMMON REACTION TO DRINKING a cold drink too fast, or sneaking up on your gray matter with a toxic alcoholic mix. Or listening to Ralph Nader give a speech. The difference is, the freeze subsides quickly with the first two.

WHAT YOU NEED

2 shots vodka

1½ shots coffee liqueur

1 shot amaretto

WHAT YOU DO

1. Combine ingredients in blender and blend on high for 5 seconds.

2. Add ice to the level of fluid in the blender. Blend on high for 30 seconds, or until completely mixed.

Quaking Landslide

everything goes topsy-turvy as your feet lose their grip on old terra firma? Hear that rumbling? Could it be? Could it be the big one? Or could it be you got no staying power—you're only on your second drink.

WHAT YOU NEED

1 shot Bailey's Irish Cream

1 shot coffee liqueur

1 shot vodka

WHAT YOU DO

1. Combine ingredients in blender. Fill with ice to level of fluid.

2. Blend on high for 1 minute or until smooth, with a uniform color.

3. Serve in highball glass.

Bartender's Syrup

A BARTENDER'S LIFE IS NOT ALL SWEETNESS and light. Matter of fact, there's a whole lot of tales of woe coming from the other side of the bar, and the bartender just has to take it. That's why sometimes a bartender's got to make his own sweetness. Once in a while, you just have to balance out the bitter tastes in life.

WHAT YOU NEED

1 cup sugar

½ cup water

WHAT YOU DO

1. Combine water and sugar in small saucepan and bring to boil.

2. Simmer syrup for 10 minutes.

3. Let cool, and refrigerate until needed.

CHAPTER 6

Feel-Better Food

Chances are, you're not going to see these recipes on *ER*. Nobody's suggesting that the right plate of stew can mend a broken bone. Or that even the most powerful chicken soup is going to correct a thyroid imbalance. It should be a matter of manly common sense that if you're bleeding profusely from anywhere, if your stomach is busy trying to exit your body, or if your fever is ringing the bell on the thermometer, you need to see a doctor. Now.

But there is that other end of the spectrum. You wake up with the sniffles. You're feeling a little punk from allergies or a little worn down from burning the candle at both ends (you're an inspiration to us all, champ). Or maybe you're just a little achy and you don't know why. When all you have is a minor complaint, quit your griping and turn to the healer of ages—good food.

Foods have long been used for their healing properties. Garlic is a natural antibiotic and can lower cholesterol. Herbs have a range of health-restoring properties. Ginger and turmeric help your immune system. It's not just the apple a day that'll keep the doctor away.

And that's not even figuring in the mental benefits of these recipes. Placebo or not, the taste of these dishes alone may change your whole outlook. Maybe you were just being a big baby, after all. We'll never tell.

Either way, next time you're feeling just a little crappy, drink plenty of fluids, get lots of rest, and visit that pharmacy you call a kitchen.

Giddyup Gazpacho

COMING TO YOU COURTESY OF SPAIN, THIS COLD soup is sometimes referred to as "liquid salad." A tasty pick-me-up just spicy enough to get your blood moving again after a long night of too much sangría, it's not so hot as to send you in search of a strong antacid. Best as a hangover cure when combined with another Spanish tradition—the midday siesta.

WHAT YOU NEED

1 large cucumber

1 medium yellow onion

2 cloves garlic

1 large celery stalk with leaves

1 28-ounce can diced tomatoes

1 small jalapeño

¼ cup parsley (about 10 sprigs)

1½ cups tomato juice or V8

1 tablespoon olive oil

½ tablespoon balsamic vinegar

Dash Worcestershire sauce

Juice of 1 lemon

Salt and pepper to taste

Tabasco to taste

WHAT YOU DO

1. Peel and seed the cucumber. Peel onion and garlic. Chop all into coarse pieces and combine in blender. Blend on medium for three 2-second bursts.

2. Place remaining ingredients in the blender (if your blender canister is too small, you'll need to do this in two batches).

3. Blend on medium in 2-second bursts, using a spatula to stir in between blending. Blend for about 15 seconds total, depending on the texture you prefer—shorter for a coarser texture, longer for a smoother soup.

4. Chill for at least 1 hour before serving.

MAKES 4 SERVINGS

THE PERFECT SERVE: Gazpacho is traditionally served with hearty, crusty bread. A dollop of sour cream on top provides a nice counterpoint to the strong flavors and spiciness in the soup.

Feel-Better Food

Kick-start Jambalaya

SHORT OF HAVING A WITCH DOCTOR FIX you up, you'll be hard-pressed to find a better way to get rid of congestion than the aromatics in this dish. One whiff and you'll finally have a good reason to shout "Bam!" But take the high road and fight the urge.

WHAT YOU NEED

2 small red onions

1 medium yellow onion

6 cloves garlic

3 scallions, trimmed

1 stick salted butter

1 large green bell pepper

1 jalapeño

1 teaspoon chili powder

½ teaspoon cayenne

½ teaspoon dried oregano

1 pound andouille sausage

¾ pound ham, cubed

1½ cups chicken broth

1 28-ounce can diced tomatoes

2 tablespoons tomato paste

2 bay leaves

2½ cups long-grain rice

WHAT YOU DO

1. Peel onions and garlic, and chop with scallions into coarse pieces. Blend on high for two 3-second bursts. Put in large pot with butter, over medium heat.

2. Seed and coarsely chop bell pepper and jalapeño. Blend on high for 3 seconds. Add to pan.

3. Blend chili powder, cayenne, and oregano on low for 5 seconds to make Creole mix. Add to pot.

4. Cover and cook until onions are soft, stirring occasionally, about 10 minutes.

5. Add sausage, ham, broth, tomatoes, paste, bay leaves, and rice. Bring mixture to boil.

6. Reduce heat to simmer and cover. Cook until rice is very tender, about 1 hour, stirring occasionally. Remove bay leaves before serving.

MAKES 4 SERVINGS

SHOP TIP: The deli department at your local grocery store will usually cube ham steaks on request, saving you the effort.

B. Bunny's Carrot Soup

RABBITS, MY GOOD MAN, RABBITS KNOW how to maintain a healthy diet. Just look at them. They hop everywhere they go. Their choppers are second to none. And, frankly, you should be so lucky as to have half the sex life of one of those furry forest dynamos.

WHAT YOU NEED

1 medium yellow onion

2 tablespoons salted butter

6 medium carrots

¼ teaspoon nutmeg

½ teaspoon dry ginger

Salt and pepper to taste

2 tablespoons long-grain rice

1½ cups chicken broth

½ teaspoon lemon zest

WHAT YOU DO

1. Peel and quarter onion. Blend on high for 3 seconds. Place in saucepan with butter, over low heat.

2. Scrub and chop carrots into coarse pieces. Blend on medium for five 3-second bursts, or until well chopped. Add to saucepan.

3. Add nutmeg, ginger, salt, and pepper to saucepan. Sauté for 5 minutes, or until onions are soft.

4. Add rice and broth to saucepan, bring to boil, then reduce to simmer. Simmer for 30 minutes or until carrots are tender.

5. Ladle soup into blender and add lemon zest. Blend on medium for 45 seconds or until soup is smooth.

MAKES 2 LARGE SERVINGS

GOOD GUY ADVICE: Don't throw out what you can't eat. Carrot soup—like most soups—can be frozen and reheated later.

Feel-Better Food

Cure-All Chicken Soup

SADLY, MOST OF US DON'T HAVE A KINDLY Jewish mother to cluck over our every complaint, cook like crazy, and tell us to "Eat, *bubbala*, eat." You'll just have to do without, and drag your sniffling, wheezing, stuffed-up carcass out of bed and into the kitchen to cook up your own cure.

WHAT YOU NEED

1 small yellow onion

3 cloves garlic

1 large celery stalk with leaves

1 large carrot

5 sprigs parsley

4 cups chicken broth

½ cup long-grain white rice

1 teaspoon dried thyme

½ teaspoon lemon zest

1 pound thin-sliced chicken cutlet

2 tablespoons olive oil

Salt and pepper to taste

WHAT YOU DO

1. Peel onion and garlic and chop into coarse pieces. Blend on high for 2 seconds.

2. Trim celery and carrot and scrub clean. Remove stems from parsley. Chop all into coarse pieces and add to blender. Blend on high for three 2-second bursts, or until vegetables are well chopped.

3. Combine blender contents with chicken broth in 2-quart saucepan, reserving ½ cup broth. Use remaining broth to rinse out blender canister, and empty into saucepan.

4. Bring to boil over high heat. Add rice, thyme, and lemon zest.

5. Reduce to simmer. While soup is simmering, coat chicken cutlets with olive oil, and sauté in skillet in 1 tablespoon of olive oil. Sauté about 5 minutes each side, or until cooked thoroughly.

6. Chop cutlets into coarse pieces, and blend on medium for five 2-second bursts, or until shredded.

7. After soup has simmered for 45 minutes, add chicken, salt, and pepper. Simmer for 15 minutes more.

MAKES 4 MODEST SERVINGS

GOOD GUY ADVICE: Learn how to properly sauté and you've added a great technique to your kitchen expertise. Here's the basic process. Preheat the sauté pan on low for about 2 minutes (to even out the effect of any "hot spots" in the pan). Then add oil or butter. Butter has more flavor, oil is less likely to burn. Add ingredients when the butter has fully melted and is slightly brown, or when the oil is hot but not sizzling. The benefit to sautéing food is that it cooks quickly and seals in moisture. That's why you should never use a fork to turn food in a sauté pan: use tongs or a spatula.

The "Regular" Granola

SEVEN NIGHTS OF PIZZA LEFT THINGS A little backed up? Get back on schedule with the help of an old friend from your hiking days—rough-and-ready granola. Start chewing on a couple fistfuls of this tasty mix and you'll be back on schedule in no time.

WHAT YOU NEED

3 cups old-fashioned oats

¼ cup sesame seeds

¼ cup flaxseeds

½ cup sunflower seeds

¼ cup wheat germ

½ cup coconut

½ cup powdered milk

½ cup peanuts

¼ cup almonds

½ cup safflower oil

¾ cup honey

2 teaspoons pure vanilla extract

½ teaspoon cinnamon

½ cup raisins

WHAT YOU DO

1. Preheat the oven to 300°F.

2. Mix first 9 ingredients in large bowl.

3. Combine safflower oil, honey, vanilla, and cinnamon in blender. Blend on medium for 15 seconds.

4. Add blender mix to dry ingredients and mix well with a fork.

5. Spread mix in a large baking pan. Bake for 50 minutes or until brown, stirring frequently.

6. Remove from oven, mix in raisins, and let cool.

MAKES ABOUT 4 CUPS

Dr. O. J.'s Shot of Pep

AS LONG AS CRYSTAL METH REMAINS illegal, and coffee cannot seriously be mainlined, you need something to get the synapses firing when you're facing an early morning meeting after an unexpected all-nighter. This sweet pick-me-up gives you the much needed, right-now blast of energy, along with a boatload of calcium and vitamin C.

WHAT YOU NEED

1 6-ounce can frozen orange juice concentrate

¼ cup water

1 cup half-and-half

¼ cup vanilla yogurt

¼ cup lemon juice

WHAT YOU DO

1. Combine orange juice and water in blender. Blend on medium for 10 seconds.

2. Add other ingredients and blend on high for 1 minute.

MAKES 1 DRINK

Stomach Settler

ENVELOPE PLEASE . . . IT'S A TAX AUDIT. THOSE aren't ants, they're termites! Your proctologist called, the colonoscopy results were lost and they need to do the test again. A day like this calls for something a little more effective than run-of-the-mill antacids.

WHAT YOU NEED

8 fresh mint leaves

2 small apples, peeled, cored, chopped, and frozen

½ cup whole milk

½ cup plain nonfat yogurt

1 teaspoon grated ginger

WHAT YOU DO

1. Crush the mint leaves using a spoon in a bowl. Combine with all ingredients in blender.

2. Blend on high for three 2-second bursts to break up apple pieces. Then blend on medium for 1 minute.

MAKES 1 DRINK

Loaded Lentil Stew

LENTILS ARE THE MICHAEL JORDAN OF legumes. Nothing can touch them for killer amounts of protein, soluble fiber, potassium, and iron. If that wasn't enough, these little disks make for a rockin' tasty stew.

WHAT YOU NEED

1 cup dry lentils

2 small carrots

2 stalks celery

1 small clove garlic

2 tablespoons salted butter

1 medium russet potato

1 tablespoon dried basil

½ teaspoon chervil

½ teaspoon cumin

⅛ teaspoon cayenne

3½ cups chicken broth

1 15-ounce can diced tomatoes

WHAT YOU DO

1. Rinse and drain lentils.

2. Scrub and chop carrots and celery into coarse pieces. Peel garlic, and blend garlic, carrots, and celery on medium for two 2-second bursts.

3. Combine in large saucepan with butter, over medium heat. Cut the potato into cubes, and add to saucepan.

4. Combine spices in blender and blend on low for 3 seconds. Add to pot and stir. Cook for 5 minutes.

5. Add lentils and broth, bring to a boil and reduce to simmer. Add tomatoes and simmer for 45 minutes.

MAKES 4 SERVINGS

Feel-Better Food

Salad Smoothie

NOTHING LIKE A REALLY GOOD STOMACH BUG— or a long night of too much everything—to give you an appreciation of the body's basic need for water and food that can be absorbed before it comes back up. If rehydration is key to you ever getting out of bed again, blend up an easily digestible mix of water-rich, nutrient-dense vegetables.

WHAT YOU NEED

1 small carrot

1 clove garlic

1 scallion, trimmed

1 medium cucumber

1 teaspoon Worcestershire sauce

1/2 teaspoon fresh lemon juice

1 cup V8

1/2 teaspoon salt

1/2 teaspoon fresh-ground pepper

Dash cayenne

8 cherry tomatoes

4 to 6 Boston lettuce leaves

WHAT YOU DO

1. Scrub, trim, and chop the carrot into coarse pieces. Peel and quarter the garlic. Combine in the blender and blend on high for two 2-second bursts.

2. Chop scallion into coarse pieces. Peel and seed cucumber and chop into coarse pieces. Combine in blender with Worcestershire sauce, lemon juice, V8, salt, pepper, and cayenne. Blend on high for five 2-second bursts, scraping down the sides as necessary.

3. Cut tomatoes in half and wash lettuce leaves. Add both to blender. Blend on medium for 30 to 40 seconds, or until well mixed, scraping down sides as necessary.

MAKES 1 LARGE SHAKE

Calming Cream of Broccoli Soup

BROCCOLI SOUP IS A favorite of superheroes far and wide. Especially Batman. Batman likes a good cream of broccoli soup for its antioxidant powers and the way it's gentle going down. So get with the program, buster. Or are you going to be the one to tell the Caped Crusader he's wrong?

WHAT YOU NEED

1 small carrot

1 large yellow onion

3 tablespoons salted butter

2 teaspoons dry mustard

½ teaspoon salt

½ teaspoon fresh-ground pepper

½ teaspoon white pepper

¼ cup Marsala

2 large heads broccoli

2 cups chicken broth

1 cup water

2 teaspoons fresh lemon juice

¼ cup sour cream

Salt and pepper to taste

WHAT YOU DO

1. Scrub carrot and peel onion. Chop both into coarse pieces and combine in blender. Blend on high for three 2-second bursts.

2. Combine onions and carrots with butter in large saucepan. Cook over medium heat for about 5 minutes, or until onions are soft.

3. Add spices and Marsala to saucepan and bring to a boil.

4. Chop stems off broccoli and chop broccoli florets into coarse pieces. Add to saucepan and reduce heat to simmer.

5. Simmer for 5 minutes and add broth and water. Bring to boil and then reduce to simmer. Simmer for 30 minutes.

6. Remove from heat and blend mix in blender, half the mix at a time. Blend on medium for 30 to 40 seconds, or until smooth. Once all the mix has been blended, return it to the large saucepan on medium heat.

7. Stir in the lemon juice, then stir in the sour cream. Add salt and pepper to taste. Serve hot.

MAKES 4 SERVINGS

Feel-Better Food

Plain Ol' Creamy Tomato Soup

IT'S NOT FLASHY EATING, but tomato soup does the trick. Tomatoes are simple, good, lycopene-rich, everyday, run-of-the-mill, feel-better food. So whether it's the sniffles or a headache, a little creamy tomato soup may be just the thing for what ails you.

WHAT YOU NEED

3 cloves peeled garlic

1 stalk celery

¼ cup olive oil

¼ teaspoon cayenne

½ teaspoon salt

½ teaspoon fresh-ground pepper

2 tablespoons all-purpose flour

½ cup Marsala

1 28-ounce can diced tomatoes

1 teaspoon sugar

¾ cup heavy cream

WHAT YOU DO

1. Chop the garlic and celery into coarse pieces and combine in blender. Blend on high for three 2-second bursts.

2. Combine garlic and celery with olive oil, cayenne, salt, and pepper in medium saucepan. Cook over medium heat for about 5 minutes. Add flour and cook 1 minute more.

3. Add Marsala and bring to a boil. Add tomatoes and sugar and reduce to simmer. Simmer covered for 35 minutes.

4. Remove the saucepan from the heat, and spoon the mix into the blender. Blend on medium for 30 seconds. (Do this in batches if your blender canister is too small.)

5. Return soup to saucepan over medium heat, and stir in cream. Serve at once.

MAKES 2 LARGE SERVINGS

Fibertastic Muffins

IF YOUR IDEA OF GETTING YOUR DAILY FIBER is dumping a spoonful of something that looks like a cross between dirt and chalk (and tastes that way too) into a glass of water, well knock yourself out, slugger. The wisest of us get all the fiber we need in super-delicious muffin form.

WHAT YOU NEED

1 cup all-purpose flour

2 teaspoons baking powder

1 teaspoon salt

1 teaspoon nutmeg

2 teaspoons cinnamon

Dash allspice

1 large apple

1 large egg

¾ cup whole milk

¼ teaspoon vanilla

½ cup canola oil

⅓ cup granulated sugar

1 cup old-fashioned oats

1 cup raisins

WHAT YOU DO

1. Preheat oven to 400°F.

2. Combine flour, baking powder, and spices in blender. Blend on low for 2 minutes. Set aside in large bowl.

3. Core, peel, and chop apple into coarse pieces. Place in blender and blend on high for three 1-second bursts. Set aside, but don't clean blender.

4. Combine egg, milk, vanilla, and oil in blender. Blend on low for 10 seconds. Add sugar and blend on medium for 15 seconds.

5. Add oats to blender and blend on medium for 5 seconds. Add apple, and blend on medium for 3 seconds.

6. Empty blender over flour mix, add raisins, and stir with large fork until the ingredients are well mixed. Spoon into nonstick muffin tins, filling each cavity three-quarters full.

7. Bake for 25 minutes. Remove muffin pan from oven and cool for 5 minutes before removing muffins.

MAKES 12 TO 14 MUFFINS

Feel-Better Food

CHAPTER 7

Sweet Treats

Please, don't pretend you haven't had those moments of weak, weak will. It's time you admitted the truth: that you've fulfilled your deviant late-night urges with canned cake frosting slathered across graham crackers, that you've actually dunked Oreos in a jar of creamy peanut butter and been blissfully happy doing it, that you have drowned a simple banana in Bosco just because you didn't think a simple banana was dessert enough. Admit it. That's the first step.

You have a sweet tooth. It happens. You're only human. Now, don't you feel better?

The trick in dealing with that empty place in your soul that cries out to be filled with sweets is to fill it with *quality* sweets. Delicious homemade treats are far more satisfying than anything you can buy at the Stop and Shop at twelve-thirty at night. And knowing that you have a whole pie to finish over time, you'll be less desperate than if you're making up your snack menu on the fly. So you'll eat less. Well, that's the theory, anyway, but it sounds nice, doesn't it?

Even if you're a total pig, and you like to follow a good dessert with a little dessert, you should make what you eat. At least then you can have a slightly better idea of what's going into your body than when you made that after-dinner salad of Ding Dongs and Ho Hos. (And by the way, that was just gross, man.)

Fudginutilicious Pie

FUDGINUTABLE GOODNESS—IT'S NOT JUST for breakfast anymore. If you're fond of those sacred foodstuffs with an unusually high fudginutable factor, then you've come to the right place. The fudginutability of this delectable pie is off the charts.

WHAT YOU NEED

½ cup pecans

1 cup granulated sugar

2 tablespoons all-purpose flour

1 tablespoon cornstarch

¼ teaspoon salt

Dash cinnamon

2 tablespoons cocoa

2 large eggs

3 tablespoons unsalted butter, melted

⅔ cup whole milk

1 teaspoon pure vanilla extract

¾ cup coconut flakes

1 9-inch pie shell, unbaked

WHAT YOU DO

1. Preheat oven to 400°F.

2. Blend pecans for five 2-second bursts on low, or until well chopped. Add other dry ingredients to blender, except for coconut, and blend on medium for 10 to 15 seconds, or until well mixed. Set aside.

3. Combine liquid ingredients in blender, and blend on medium for 15 seconds.

4. With blender running, add dry ingredients. Finally, add coconut and blend for 10 seconds more, or until completely integrated. Scrape down sides and stir mix as necessary.

5. Pour mix into pie shell. Bake for 30 minutes, or until a knife inserted in the center comes out clean. Let cool for 5 minutes before serving.

MAKES 6 TO 8 SLICES

GOOD GUY ADVICE: When slicing pies and other baked goods, run hot water over the knife between every cut, to ensure the cleanest cuts. For dense cakes such as cheesecake, you can use fine dental floss held very tight.

Aunt Macy's Magic Coconut Custard Pie

AUNT MACY WAS WAY COOL. SHE COULD PLAY the guitar, pull coins out of your ear, and make a pie that formed its own crust. She'd blend it up, pour it in a pie pan, say the magic words over the oven, and presto! Out it would come with crust in place. And if you still think it was magic, you are one sad clown.

WHAT YOU NEED

⅔ cup all-purpose flour

¼ teaspoon salt

½ teaspoon baking powder

4 large eggs

1¾ cups whole milk

¼ cup heavy cream

1 teaspoon pure vanilla extract

4 tablespoons salted butter, softened

¾ cup granulated sugar

Dash cinnamon

¼ teaspoon nutmeg

1 cup shredded coconut

WHAT YOU DO

1. Preheat oven to 350°F.

2. Combine flour, salt, and baking powder in blender. Blend on medium for 2 minutes. Set aside.

3. Combine eggs, milk, cream, vanilla, and butter in blender and blend on low for 30 seconds, or until thoroughly mixed. Add sugar, cinnamon, and nutmeg, and blend on medium for 10 seconds.

4. Add coconut to blender and blend on low for 10 seconds. Leave the blender running, and slowly pour in flour mixture.

5. Pour into 2 nonstick 9-inch pie pans. Bake for 1 hour.

6. Let cool for 5 to 10 minutes on wire rack, and eat warm. Refrigerate after cooling.

MAKES 8 TO 12 LARGE SLICES

A MAN'S WHIRLED

GOOD GUY ADVICE: In a pinch, the savvy guy knows how to substitute what's on hand for what he needs. When you're out of heavy cream, substitute ¾ cup whole milk mixed with ¼ cup melted butter per 1 cup of heavy cream. You can substitute granulated sugar for light or dark brown sugar, although the caramel taste will be lost. Substitute a mix of ½ granulated white and ½ dark brown sugar to make the equivalent of light brown sugar. If your hot fudge sundae binge left you short on unsweetened chocolate, use 3 tablespoons of cocoa to 1 tablespoon of vegetable oil to replace an ounce of unsweetened chocolate for baking.

PBJ Spin

IF THERE WAS ANY JUSTICE IN THIS WORLD, YOU COULD pick peanut-butter-and-jelly sandwiches off bushes growing in the wild. But in an unjust and cruel world, you need to set things right in whatever ways you can. Adding a little ice cream to a time-tested favorite seems as good a way as any.

WHAT YOU NEED

1½ tablespoons creamy peanut butter

1½ tablespoons strawberry jam

½ cup whole milk

2 heaping scoops premium vanilla ice cream, softened

WHAT YOU DO

1. Combine peanut butter, jelly, and milk in blender and blend on high for 15 seconds.

2. Add ice cream and blend on medium for three 2-second bursts. Then blend on high for 15 to 20 seconds, or until smooth.

MAKES 1 LARGE SHAKE

Poppy's Lemon Poppy Seed Bread

OKAY, THIS ONE requires a warning. It may seem like a simple little treat, but this stuff is addictive. It's even more addictive than *Law & Order*. Look, really, proceed with caution. If Poppy had only known what he was creating, I don't think he ever would have stepped into the kitchen.

WHAT YOU NEED

Bread

1½ cups all-purpose flour

1 teaspoon baking powder

½ teaspoon salt

1 stick unsalted butter, softened almost to melting

1 cup granulated sugar

2 large eggs

2 tablespoons poppy seeds

2 teaspoons lemon zest

⅓ cup whole milk

Glaze

½ cup confectioners' sugar

¼ cup lemon juice, or the juice of 1 large lemon

WHAT YOU DO

Bread

1. Preheat oven to 350°F. Grease a 9 by 5-inch loaf pan.

2. Combine flour, baking powder, and salt in blender, and blend on medium for 2 minutes. Set aside in large bowl.

3. Combine butter and sugar in blender, and begin blending on low. As the ingredients start to mix, add eggs, poppy seeds, and lemon zest. Stop and scrape down ingredients as necessary.

4. When the ingredients in the blender are combined, add milk. Blend on medium for 20 seconds or until smooth.

5. Empty blender over flour mix, and stir together with large fork until well blended.

6. Pour the mix into the loaf pan, and bake for 50 minutes, or until a knife inserted into the center comes out clean.

7. Remove and cool on a wire rack for 15 minutes. Use a knife to gently free the sides of the bread from the pan, and remove the loaf.

8. Put the bread on a sheet of aluminum foil, poke several holes along the top of the loaf, and coat with glaze, pouring the glaze slowly along the crown of the loaf.

Glaze

1. Combine sugar and lemon juice in blender and blend on low for 15 to 20 seconds, or until smooth and well mixed.

2. Pour slowly over bread. Let harden before slicing.

MAKES 6 TO 8 THICK SLICES

GOOD GUY ADVICE: You'll find poppy seeds in the spice aisle. Refrigerate after use, because the little buggers can go bad.

Sweet Treats

Chocolate Chip Banana Loaf

YOU MAY NOT SPEND YOUR nights dreaming about banana bread, but that's just your mind being busy with other things. If it had its way, it would spend all day thinking about banana bread. And the only thing better than banana bread is banana bread that's just filthy with chocolate chips. There. Now let's see what you dream about.

WHAT YOU NEED

2 cups all-purpose flour

1 teaspoon baking powder

½ teaspoon baking soda

1 teaspoon salt

1 stick unsalted butter, softened

2 large eggs

1 cup mashed ripe banana
(2 to 3 medium)

½ teaspoon vanilla

¼ teaspoon nutmeg

1 cup granulated sugar

1 cup semisweet chocolate chips

WHAT YOU DO

1. Preheat oven to 350°F. Grease bottom of a 9-by-5-inch loaf pan.

2. Combine flour, baking powder and soda, and salt in blender. Blend on medium for 2 minutes, and set aside in large bowl.

3. Combine butter, eggs, banana, and vanilla in blender, and blend on medium for 1 minute. Stop to scrape down sides as necessary.

4. Add nutmeg and slowly add sugar to blender and blend on medium for 15 seconds.

5. Empty blender over flour mix. Cover with chocolate chips and stir together with a large fork, until well mixed.

6. Pour batter into pan, and bake for 1 hour, or until knife inserted in center comes out clean.

7. Remove from oven, cool 10 minutes, and carefully remove from pan. Cool completely on wire rack.

MAKES ABOUT 6 TO 8 THICK SLICES

GOOD GUY ADVICE: Even in baking, location is everything. For best results, place anything you bake as close as possible to center of the oven. And don't open the oven door for the first half of the baking time or the air you introduce into the oven may retard how the baked goods rise.

Chocolate Puff

SOMEWHERE BETWEEN THE HOMEY, TONGUE-HUGGING texture of chocolate birthday cake and the smooth richness of chocolate mousse lies the chocolate puff. It's not a soufflé, it's not pudding, and it isn't really all that puffy. But it is delicious. Chocolately delicious. And is there any better kind of delicious?

WHAT YOU NEED

2 ounces unsweetened chocolate

1 teaspoon cocoa

1 cup whole milk

3 slices white bread, crusts removed

¾ cup granulated sugar

1 tablespoon unsalted butter, softened

1 teaspoon pure vanilla extract

¼ teaspoon salt

4 large eggs, separated

WHAT YOU DO:

1. Preheat oven to 350°F.

2. Break chocolate up into blender and add cocoa. Heat the milk until it is scalding, but not boiling. Pour hot milk over the chocolate and blend on low for 15 seconds.

3. Tear up the bread and add to the blender, along with the sugar, butter, vanilla, and salt. Blend on medium for 20 seconds, or until smooth.

4. Add egg yolks and blend for 15 seconds on medium. Set mixture aside in a bowl and thoroughly clean blender canister.

5. Blend egg whites for 4 minutes on low. Fold in chocolate mixture and blend on medium for 1 minute.

6. Pour mix into 4 ramekins, or a single 2-quart casserole dish. Bake for 1 hour. Turn oven off and open door to cool.

7. Remove after 5 minutes, and let cool an additional 10 to 15 minutes before serving.

MAKES 4 SERVINGS

THE PERFECT SERVE: You might think it's hard to improve on this chocolate beauty, and you're right. But a little coating of sprinkled confectioners' sugar couldn't hurt and makes the presentation a little nicer. Or add a touch of flair when you're trying to impress somebody by serving Dreamy Chambord Cream (page 138) on the side.

Decadence Cake

DECADENCE IS IN, JUST ASK DONALD TRUMP. DON'T be left out of this trend, or you'll be crying a river of tears when deprivation and temperance make a comeback. No, you don't want to have regrets. Take advantage of an orgy of chocolate cake, chocolate topping, and ripe strawberries while you still can.

WHAT YOU NEED

¾ cup toasted almonds

¼ teaspoon cinnamon

5 tablespoons cocoa powder

1 stick unsalted butter, softened almost to melting

4 large eggs

¾ teaspoon pure vanilla extract

¾ cup granulated sugar

3 tablespoons light brown sugar

10 large, ripe strawberries

½ cup semisweet chocolate chips

½ teaspoon orange zest

¼ cup heavy cream

WHAT YOU DO

1. Preheat oven to 350°F.

2. Combine almonds, cinnamon, and cocoa powder in blender, and blend on high for five to seven 2-second bursts, or until finely ground. Set aside.

3. Combine butter, eggs, vanilla, and orange zest in blender. Blend on high for 10 seconds. Add sugars and blend on low for 1 minute. Scrape down and stir as necessary to keep the mix blending.

4. Chop 6 strawberries into coarse pieces. Add almond mix and chopped strawberries to blender, and blend on low for 1 minute. Stop and scrape down sides as necessary.

5. Pour the mix into an 8-inch springform pan. Bake for 40 minutes, or until a knife inserted in the center comes out clean.

6. Remove from oven and let cool on a wire rack for 30 minutes. Carefully remove from pan with a knife when cool.

7. Place chocolate chips in blender, and heat cream in saucepan over medium heat until hot but not boiling. Add to blender and blend on low for 30 to 45 seconds, stopping as necessary to scrape down unmelted chips. Blend until smooth.

8. Pour chocolate sauce over cake, moving canister in slow circles as you pour to spread the chocolate evenly. Smooth surface with a knife. Let chocolate cool.

9. Thinly slice remaining strawberries, and place slices in rows on top of cake.

MAKES 6 TO 8 SERVINGS

GOOD GUY ADVICE: A springform pan is not an Olympic dive. It's a special cake pan with a latched side that can be opened—or sprung—after baking, to quickly, easily, and completely separate the sides of the cake from the sides of the pan.

OUTSTANDING OPTIONS: If you can't find toasted almonds, buy untoasted and make your own. Put the nuts on a baking sheet or in a large baking pan, and place in an oven preheated to 350°F. Toast for about 7 to 10 minutes, stirring or turning the nuts as they toast. The nuts don't need to radically change color, but you should notice a strong pleasant almond odor as the nuts become toasted. Better to remove them early than risk burning. Put the nuts on a dish towel to cool, then chop to desired consistency using the blender.

Sweet, Sweet Caramel Sauce

MAN, EVERY SO OFTEN YOU just have to have that over-the-top sweet, the kind of sweet that makes your teeth ache, sweet that will satisfy your sugar craving at the cellular level. At times like that, put that diet book deep in a drawer and break out this ice-cream-topping, super sugar freakout.

WHAT YOU NEED

⅔ cup dark brown sugar

¼ teaspoon salt

½ teaspoon pure vanilla extract

2 tablespoons salted butter, softened almost to melting

½ cup heavy cream

WHAT YOU DO

1. Combine sugar, salt, vanilla, and butter in blender.

2. Heat cream in saucepan over medium heat until scalding but not boiling. Pour over ingredients in blender and blend on high for 20 seconds.

3. Let cool for 3 to 5 minutes before serving.

MAKES ENOUGH FOR 6 ICE CREAM SUNDAES

THE PERFECT SERVE: A little of this sweet sauce goes a long way. Use about 1 tablespoon per scoop of ice cream. If you use it right away, it will be very liquid. If you prefer a thicker sauce, let it cool for 15 to 20 minutes.

Marvelous Very Blueberry Muffins

THE ONLY THING better than a morning cup of coffee and a delicious breakfast muffin is a muffin filled with healthy, juicy, tasty berries. Suddenly, even workday mornings are a cause to celebrate.

WHAT YOU NEED

2 cups all-purpose flour

3 teaspoons baking powder

Dash cinnamon

½ teaspoon salt

2 cups large, ripe blueberries

2 large eggs

4 tablespoons unsalted butter, softened

¼ teaspoon vanilla

¼ cup heavy cream

¾ cup whole milk

¾ cup granulated sugar

WHAT YOU DO

1. Preheat oven to 400°F.

2. Combine flour, baking powder, cinnamon, and salt in blender. Blend on low for 2 minutes. Set aside.

3. Mix blueberries into dry mix well (but being careful not to squish the berries).

4. Combine eggs, butter, vanilla, cream, and milk in blender. Blend on high for 30 seconds, or until thoroughly mixed. Add sugar and blend on medium for 1 minute.

5. Empty blender into dry mixture and stir with large fork until ingredients are combined. Don't overstir or stir too vigorously, or blueberries will burst. Spoon into greased muffin tins, filling each cavity two-thirds full.

6. Bake for 25 to 30 minutes, or until puffed and golden brown. Remove and let cool. Remove muffins from tins after they are completely cool.

MAKES 10 TO 12 MUFFINS

GOOD GUY ADVICE: Even if you have nonstick muffin tins, it's a good idea to grease them. Use a paper towel (or the leftover wrapping from a softened stick of butter) to wipe a light coat of butter or shortening around the inside of the tins' cavities. If you want the puffy rounded top like bakeries have on their muffins, grease the bottom and about halfway up the sides of the cavities. You can save yourself a little cleanup by using muffin liners, available in the baking section of your local supermarket. But liners are definitely old school and better used for cupcakes.

Right Now Brownies

THERE'S A MOMENT IN EVERY DAY—SIXTY of them in each hour, to be exact—that cries out for a perfect brownie. At those moments, you have to admit, in your heart of hearts, that there just isn't a wrong time for a chewy, fudgy brownie—except for "later."

WHAT YOU NEED

1 cup all-purpose flour

1 teaspoon baking powder

½ teaspoon salt

4 large eggs

1 teaspoon heavy cream

1¼ cups granulated sugar

2 teaspoons pure vanilla extract

2 sticks unsalted butter

1½ cups semisweet chocolate chips

Dash cinnamon

½ teaspoon cocoa

WHAT YOU DO

1. Preheat oven to 350°F. Grease a square 9-inch baking pan, and then line the bottom and edges with waxed paper, and grease the paper.

2. Combine flour, baking powder, and salt in blender. Blend on medium for 2 minutes. Set aside in large bowl.

3. Combine eggs, cream, sugar, and vanilla in blender, in that order. Blend on medium for 5 seconds, then increase to high for 20 to 30 seconds. Set mix aside.

4. Melt butter in saucepan over medium heat. Place chocolate chips in blender. Pour butter over chocolate while blending on low. Blend on medium for 15 seconds, or until smooth. Add cinnamon and cocoa and blend on medium for 5 seconds more.

5. Slowly add egg mixture to blender, blending on medium for 30 seconds. Your blender may clog on the mix. Stop and mix with spoon, and then continue blending on medium until well mixed.

6. Combine in large mixing bowl with flour mixture and stir together with a large fork, until evenly mixed.

7. Spread batter into baking pan. Bake for 45 minutes. Remove pan to wire rack until completely cool.

8. Pull brownies out of pan and remove paper from bottom and sides of brownies. Cut into squares for serving.

MAKES ABOUT 12 TO 14 CHEWY BROWNIES

OUTSTANDING OPTIONS: If you like nuts, add 1 cup to the mix in step 6. If you're not down with the chewy texture of this brownie, you can make it more cakelike by adding 5 to 10 minutes to the bake time.

Holy Hot Fudge Topping

COME PRAY AT THE ALTAR OF CHOCOLATE divinity. Bow down before the sacred sauce that miraculously transforms any bowl of simple ice cream into an otherworldly delight beyond imagination. Bow down, mortal, because you are not worthy.

WHAT YOU NEED

¾ cup heavy cream

1 12-ounce package unsweetened chocolate chips

1 tablespoon cocoa

¾ cup granulated sugar

1 teaspoon pure vanilla extract

Dash salt

WHAT YOU DO

1. Heat the cream until very hot but not boiling.

2. Combine other ingredients in blender and pour cream over them. Blend on medium for 15 seconds, or until completely mixed.

3. Let cool for 3 minutes, and serve over ice cream, or keep warm in a metal bowl in a pan of hot water.

MAKES TOPPING FOR 2 LARGE SUNDAES

GOOD GUY ADVICE: Chocolate chips are the best option for blending, but the finest premium chocolate comes in bar form. If you choose to use this type of chocolate, take the 1-ounce bars and double-bag them in plastic sandwich bags. Put them on a hard, stable surface (a concrete garage floor or patio works great) and pound with a mallet or cast iron pot.

Soul-Satisfying Oatmeal Raisin Cookies

SOMEWHERE DEEP INSIDE, THE INNER child in all of us is asking for just a few of these gems. Just a few. You and I know that little boy or girl isn't going to settle for a few, but it's nice that he or she asked. Won't you reward that angelic inner child before the damn thing makes you buy that red convertible BMW?

WHAT YOU NEED

1¼ cups all-purpose flour

1 teaspoon baking soda

1 teaspoon cinnamon

Dash nutmeg

¼ teaspoon ground cloves

½ teaspoon salt

2 sticks unsalted butter, softened

3 large eggs

1 teaspoon pure vanilla extract

¼ cup cream

1 cup firmly packed light brown sugar

½ cup granulated sugar

2½ cups old-fashioned oats

1 cup raisins

WHAT YOU DO

1. Preheat oven to 350°F.

2. Combine flour, baking soda, and spices in blender. Blend on low for 2 minutes, or until well mixed. Set aside in large mixing bowl.

3. Combine butter, eggs, vanilla, cream, and sugars, in that order, and blend on low for 1 minute, scraping down the sides as necessary.

4. Empty egg mix into bowl of dry ingredients. Add oats and raisins and use a large fork to mix thoroughly.

5. Drop by spoonfuls onto a nonstick baking sheet. Bake 10 to 12 minutes, or until golden brown. Cool on wire rack.

MAKES ABOUT 30 COOKIES

GOOD GUY ADVICE: We'd all like to think that there's no such thing as too many cookies, but even the heartiest man among us has his limits. If you have too many cookies on hand and fear that they will go stale, freeze some. When you're ready for another cookie feast, just pull them out and let them defrost at room temperature. Double-bag in zipper lock refrigerator bags. They'll be good for up to 4 weeks.

Strawberry Fields Chiffon Pie

THE BEST THING TO EVER happen to strawberries was to find their way into this light-as-air, fluffy-as-a-pillow, stomach ecstasy dream pie. If there is a shining pinnacle of strawberryhood, a Mount Olympus for strawberries, surely this is it.

WHAT YOU NEED

¼ cup whole milk

1 envelope unflavored gelatin

½ cup granulated sugar

¼ cup half-and-half, heated

1 teaspoon pure vanilla extract

Dash cinnamon

1 cup frozen strawberries, thawed

2 large eggs

⅓ teaspoon lemon zest

1½ 8-ounce packages cream cheese, softened and cut up into cubes

½ cup heavy cream

9-inch graham cracker crust, prebaked

WHAT YOU DO

1. Combine milk and gelatin in blender, and blend on high for 5 seconds.

2. Add sugar and heated half-and-half. Blend on high 5 seconds.

3. Add vanilla, cinnamon, strawberries, eggs, and lemon zest, and blend on high for 10 seconds.

4. Let blender continue to run, and add cream cheese and heavy cream. Blend 30 seconds, or until smooth.

5. Pour into prebaked 9-inch graham cracker crust. Chill until firm, about 1 hour.

MAKES 4 TO 6 SERVINGS

SHOP TIP: Find gelatin packets in the juice aisle and prebaked pie crusts in the baking section of your local grocery store.

Sweet Treats

Lip-smacking Lemon Bars

THE LEMON GROWERS OF AMERICA worked so damn hard to give us a bumper crop of the sour yellow "official fruit of the pucker" that we had to give them a dessert worthy of their efforts. This is for you guys, each and every one of you.

WHAT YOU NEED

Crust

1¼ cups all-purpose flour

⅓ cup confectioners' sugar

¼ teaspoon salt

2 tablespoons cornstarch

2 sticks unsalted butter, softened to room temperature

Lemon Filling

4 large eggs

1½ cups granulated sugar

3 tablespoons all-purpose flour

2 teaspoons lemon zest

1 cup fresh lemon juice, strained

⅛ teaspoon salt

WHAT YOU DO

Crust

1. Lightly butter an 8-inch square baking pan and line it with a sheet of waxed paper with ends draping over the edge of the pan by 1 inch or more. Lightly grease the waxed paper.

2. Combine flour, confectioners' sugar, salt, and cornstarch in blender, and blend on medium for 1 minute.

3. Cut butter into 12 to 14 chunks, and combine in a large bowl with flour mix. Mash together with large fork, until mix is the texture of a coarse meal.

4. Spread mixture into baking pan. Use a spoon to press crust firmly into place, in an even layer across the pan and about ½ inch up the sides. Regularly clean off the back of the spoon and coat it with flour to make the process easier.

5. Preheat oven to 350°F. Refrigerate crust for 30 minutes.

6. Remove chilled crust and bake for about 20 minutes, or until golden brown.

Filling

1. While crust is baking, combine eggs, granulated sugar, and flour in blender. Blend on medium for 10 seconds.

2. Add lemon zest, lemon juice, and salt. Blend on medium for 20 seconds.

3. Remove crust from oven, and reduce oven temperature to 325°F. Pour lemon mix over warm crust.

4. Bake for 30 minutes, or until filling is firm to the touch.

5. Remove pan and cool on wire rack for at least 30 minutes, or until room temperature.

6. Grasp the edges of the bottom layer of waxed paper and lift the lemon bars out.

7. Carefully peel the paper down from the sides and slice into bars. Wipe knife clean between cuts.

MAKES 18 TO 20 BARS

THE PERFECT SERVE: A sprinkle of confectioners' sugar over top of the bars cuts the tart taste and gives them a nice look.

Watermelon Snow

SNOW IN JULY? EVERY KID'S FANTASY COMES to life with this amazingly simple hot-weather treat. And let's be real here, just because you're too old for a Stingray, doesn't mean you don't still entertain childhood fantasies.

WHAT YOU NEED

2 cups seedless watermelon chunks

6 tablespoons granulated sugar

¼ cup water

¼ teaspoon lemon juice

WHAT YOU DO

1. Combine ingredients and blend on medium for 15 seconds. Pour into plastic container.

2. Freeze just until edges are firm, about 30 minutes. Spoon snow into blender canister and blend on medium until fluffy.

3. Return snow to freezer and freeze solid. Remove a few minutes before serving.

MAKES 4 SERVINGS

Gingerbread, Man

THERE AIN'T NO BREAD LIKE GINGERBREAD. If you thought those stiff holiday figures were what gingerbread was all about, you don't know Jack (and you sure as heck don't know gingerbread). This version is good all year long, sweet and spicy all at once. And you don't have to paint frosting buttons on this one.

WHAT YOU NEED

½ cup whole milk

1 tablespoon fresh lemon juice

1 teaspoon chopped candied ginger

1½ cups all-purpose flour

½ teaspoon baking soda

2 teaspoons ground dried ginger

1 teaspoon cinnamon

½ teaspoon ground cloves

½ teaspoon salt

¼ teaspoon allspice

1 teaspoon lemon zest

½ cup firmly packed dark brown sugar

½ teaspoon fresh-grated ginger

2 large eggs

½ cup unsulfured molasses

1 stick unsalted butter, melted and cooled

WHAT YOU DO

1. Preheat the oven to 350°F.

2. Grease a square 8-inch baking pan and dust it with flour.

3. Mix milk and lemon juice together in small bowl, so that the milk curdles.

4. Blend candied ginger on high for 2 seconds. Add flour, baking soda, dried ginger, cinnamon, cloves, salt, and allspice to blender, and blend on medium for 2 minutes. Set aside.

5. Combine milk mix, lemon zest, sugar, fresh ginger, eggs, molasses, and butter in blender. Blend on medium for 30 seconds, or until smooth.

6. Add the dry mix to the blender, while blending on medium. The mixer may slow. Mix for 1 minute, stopping regularly to scrape down the sides and stir the mix.

7. Pour the batter into the baking pan and bake 25 to 30 minutes, or until the top is puffed and dry, and the sides begin to pull away from the pan. Cool completely on a wire rack before removing gingerbread from pan and cutting into squares.

MAKES 12 SQUARES

THE PERFECT SERVE: Dress up your gingerbread with a light sprinkle of confectioners' sugar or a dollop of Homespun Cream on the side.

Homespun Cream

SOME FOODS PROVIDE VITAL NUTRIENTS. SOME foods are sources of essential minerals. Some foods offer all the fiber you'll need in a day. Some foods lower serum cholesterol when eaten in volume. And then some foods, a very rare few, nourish the soul. 'Nuff said.

WHAT YOU NEED

½ cup heavy cream

¼ teaspoon pure vanilla extract

1 teaspoon sugar

WHAT YOU DO

1. Combine ingredients in blender.

2. Blend on medium for 12 to 15 seconds, or until the cream is stiff.

MAKES 2 LARGE SERVINGS

OUTSTANDING OPTIONS: Unsweetened whipped cream is a more sophisticated alternative for very sweet desserts. Leave out the sugar and show your panache.

Sweet Treats

Dreamy Chambord Cream

IF YOUR STOMACH HAD AN imagination, if your tongue could fantasize, if your throat had just one wish, they would all conjure up Dreamy Chambord Cream. Whipped cream's richer, prettier cousin, this accompaniment to desserts small and large is surely the product of a fairy godchef.

WHAT YOU NEED

¾ cup heavy cream

3 drops pure vanilla extract

1 teaspoon Chambord liqueur

½ teaspoon granulated sugar

WHAT YOU DO

1. Combine ingredients in blender.

2. Blend on medium for 7 to 10 seconds, or just until cream begins to stiffen. It should still be slightly liquid when served.

MAKES 4 SERVINGS

SHOP TIP: Chambord is a rich, black raspberry liqueur. Use it sparingly—a little goes a long way. Unless you are planning on making a lot of desserts that call for this cream, buy a miniature "airplane-size" bottle from your local liquor store.

CHAPTER 8

Liquid Vim and Vigor

It's a fast-paced world out there, hombre. The path to the corner office is paved with eighty-hour weeks, and the demands of day-to-day life are more stressful than ever. Your boss wants results. Your significant other wants results. You go to the gym three times a week and you want results. What's the result? A lot of pressure and little time to make healthy sit-down meals.

Once again, blender to the rescue.

In about the time it takes to catch the morning weather and traffic, you can mix up a powerful blend full of health-enhancing ingredients. What better way to get vital nutrients than in a tasty shake? Until they make a Willy Wonka meal in a pill, smoothies are as handy as it gets.

And these smoothies don't fall short in the flavor department, because quick gulp or not, you don't want anything leaving a bad taste in your mouth.

But just so we're clear: None of these elixirs is the magic bullet that's going to solve all your health issues past, present, and future. There is no cure-all in a glass. These are just boosts (like the nitrous setup you put in your '69 Firebird back in college) to your diet. They are part of a good diet and exercise plan, not a substitute. And just so you know, each recipe equals 1 ample shake, except where noted.

So eat right, buddy. Go to the gym. Breathe. Take care of yourself. See a doctor once a year. And, in between, help yourself out with these quick-mix health boosters.

Protein Power Slammer

IF YOU'RE TRYING TO PUT ON SOME Charles Atlas poundage, or are pumping iron for any reason, you need to give your muscles loads of protein so that they can repair and rebuild themselves. This blend not only supplies lots of muscle fuel, it also offers chromium and magnesium—minerals essential for getting that fuel to your muscles.

WHAT YOU NEED

1 cup skim milk

2 tablespoons reduced-fat creamy peanut butter

2 teaspoons wheat germ

1 banana, sliced and frozen

1 tablespoon soy protein powder

WHAT YOU DO

1. Combine first 3 ingredients and blend on high for 3 seconds.

2. Add banana and protein powder and blend on high for 1 minute.

LINEUP SUBSTITUTIONS: This recipe uses soy protein powder, which is a natural, plant-based protein source, but you can opt for other types of protein powder. Just read labels carefully because many products include additives you may not want. Whatever brand you choose, you can vary the flavor in the recipe by selecting flavored varieties—chocolate or vanilla go best with the peanut butter in this shake.

Liquid vim and vigor

Cancer-Busting Cocktail

NOBODY LIKES TO THINK ABOUT THE big C, but in this world, hiding your head in the sand is a recipe for disaster. Prevention is key, and this veggie-heavy mixture is all about liquid prevention. It's full of indole-3-carbinol, phytochemicals, and antioxidants that throw some serious hurt on those evil free radicals.

WHAT YOU NEED

1 teaspoon flaxseed

1 small head broccoli (about ½ cup florets)

¼ teaspoon chopped jalapeño

¼ ripe avocado

¼ cup chopped kale leaves

2 cups tomato juice

Salt and pepper to taste

WHAT YOU DO

1. Blend the flaxseed on high for three 2-second bursts, or until pulverized.

2. Chop the stems off the broccoli and discard. Combine with remaining ingredients in blender. Blend on low for 15 seconds, then on high for 1 minute.

3. Taste and add salt and pepper as desired for flavor.

Heart-Healthy Nut Drink

RIGHT ABOUT NOW, YOU'RE SCRATCHING your head saying, "But nuts have fat," and you're right, Dr. Welby. Lots of good fats and omega-3 oils that are going to work along with the fish-oil tocopherols to keep your ticker in shape. All wrapped in a tangy, tomato taste.

WHAT YOU NEED

¼ cup walnuts

1 teaspoon flaxseed

¼ small yellow onion, peeled

2 teaspoons fish oil

1 cup tomato juice

Lemon juice or fresh-ground pepper to taste

WHAT YOU DO

1. Combine walnuts and flaxseed in blender and blend on high for five 2-second bursts.

2. Add onion to blender and blend on high for 3 seconds. Add fish oil and tomato juice and blend on low for 10 seconds, then high for 2 minutes.

3. Add a splash of lemon juice or fresh-ground pepper to taste.

SHOP TIP: Buy fish oil at your local health food store. Get the smallest container you can buy because you only use a little at a time. Take advantage of the many coronary benefits by adding ½ teaspoon of fish oil any time you use olive or vegetable oil in a savory dish such as spaghetti sauce.

Liquid vim and vigor

Power Prostate Tea Punch

IT'S A PRETTY CLEAR CHOICE: Take care of your prostate now or pay the price later on. And lest you forget, the P-gland also plays a critical part in sexual function. If you want to go the distance, keep things shipshape downstairs.

WHAT YOU NEED

½ orange

1 cup brewed green tea, chilled

½ cup real cranberry juice

1 tablespoon lemon juice

1 saw palmetto 160-milligram powder capsule

WHAT YOU DO

1. Peel and remove the pith from the orange. Freeze separated quarters.

2. Brew tea and let it steep for 3 minutes. Chill in refrigerator.

3. Combine all ingredients in blender, and blend on high for two 2-second bursts to break down orange quarters. Blend on high 1 to 2 minutes, or until completely smooth.

Quick-Burst Energy Blast

TAKE A LITTLE ACCESSIBLE glucose, combine it with a few beneficial complex carbs, add a touch of natural protein and you've got an energy shake that's a heck of lot healthier for you than a double latte. Now get back to work, tiger.

WHAT YOU NEED

1 cup orange juice

¼ cup lime juice

½ cup whole, frozen strawberries (about 5)

½ banana

¼ cup silken tofu

1 tablespoon honey

WHAT TO DO

1. Combine ingredients in blender.

2. Blend on medium for 5 seconds, or until ingredients begin to combine, then switch to high and blend for 1 minute.

GOOD GUY ADVICE: The silken tofu in this recipe is included mostly for the smooth texture it adds, but this high-protein food offers big health benefits like lowering cholesterol and fighting bone problems. You can use it as a substitute in smoothie recipes calling for plain yogurt.

Sports Performance Guzzle

SWEAT'S LIKE A WITHDRAWAL ON the bank account that is your body's electrolytes. Man's got to make some deposits if he wants to keep a balanced account. Replace critical fluids, glucose, and salts with this home brew that tastes a little like the power potions hawked by all those pro athletes.

WHAT YOU NEED

1 package unsweetened Kool-Aid (any flavor)

4 cups cold water

½ cup granulated sugar

½ teaspoon salt

½ cup orange juice

1 teaspoon lemon juice

WHAT YOU DO

1. Combine Kool-Aid and water in blender, and blend on high for 5 seconds.

2. Add other ingredients and blend on high for 15 to 20 seconds, or until well mixed.

3. Chill in plastic bottles until needed.

MAKES ABOUT ½ GALLON OF DRINK

Liquid Vim and Vigor

Craving-Curing Smoothie

DRINK IT FOR THE SPICY APPLE CIDER taste, but relish it for the 1 gram of fat, and the blood-sugar-leveling properties that keep cravings under control and your energy on an even keel. There may be carbs, but they're good carbs.

WHAT YOU NEED

1 small McIntosh apple, cored and peeled

3 tablespoons nonfat plain yogurt

2 tablespoons unsweetened applesauce

½ teaspoon cinnamon

½ teaspoon pure vanilla extract

½ cup all-natural apple juice

¼ teaspoon ground nutmeg

WHAT YOU DO

1. Chop the apple into coarse pieces and freeze.

2. Combine yogurt and applesauce in blender. Blend on high for 10 seconds.

3. Add frozen apple, cinnamon, vanilla, apple juice, and nutmeg. Blend on medium for 10 seconds, or until apple is thoroughly chopped, and then blend on high for 1 minute.

A MAN'S WHIRLED

Refreshing Morning Swig

IS THE ENGINE A LITTLE SLOW TO start in the morning? Maybe what you need is a refreshing A.M. fruity zing. This is like an alarm clock for the inside of your head, with a taste that will start the day off right. We even threw in some mint, just in case your mouthwash needs reinforcement. Off you go, then.

WHAT YOU NEED

½ cup frozen green grapes

½ kiwi

1 slice Bosc pear

6 large mint leaves

¼ cup lemon juice

½ cup unsweetened pineapple juice

WHAT YOU DO

1. Take the grapes out of the freezer and let them thaw just a little.

2. Peel the kiwi and cut the kiwi and pear into coarse chunks.

3. Combine all the ingredients in the blender, crushing the mint leaves right before you add them.

4. Blend on medium for 10 seconds, and then blend on high for 1 minute or until completely smooth.

Bone-Building Slurp

THIS CREAMY, DREAMY SMOOTHIE IS ALL about calcium—over 100 percent of the daily requirement. And that's not just good news for your bones; calcium helps keep your choppers in good shape, and plays a role in heart health.

WHAT YOU NEED

2 bananas, peeled, sliced, and frozen

1 cup whole milk

1 cup nonfat vanilla yogurt

1 cup orange juice

WHAT YOU DO

1. Combine ingredients and blend on medium for 10 seconds.

2. Blend on high for 1 minute.

Mighty Mental Mix

IT MAY SEEM LIKE AN ODD COMBINATION of ingredients, but it tastes good! This shake is loaded with potassium and other minerals necessary for keeping the synapses firing like a well-tuned car, along with heaps of choline, essential if you're going to remember where you put your keys.

WHAT YOU NEED

1 small apple, cored and peeled

¼ cup fresh spinach (about 5 leaves)

½ stalk celery

½ yellow bell pepper

1 teaspoon flaxseed

1 cup skim milk

1 tablespoon creamy peanut butter

½ large ripe banana

WHAT YOU DO

1. Chop the apple into coarse pieces and freeze.

2. Wash the spinach leaves. Chop the celery and bell pepper into coarse pieces.

3. Blend flaxseed on high for three 2-second bursts.

4. Combine all the ingredients in the blender. Blend on medium for 10 seconds, or until ingredients are chopped into small pieces. Blend on high for 1 minute.

Plumbing Health Mix

WHEN THE PIPES DON'T WORK, THE WHOLE house falls apart. That's why you need to keep your plumbing in good repair with a cocktail full of zinc and other infection-fighting agents. And the diuretic properties of these juices help keep the hydraulics busy as they should be.

WHAT YOU NEED

1 small apple, cored, chopped, and frozen

½ cup pure cranberry juice

½ cup low-fat vanilla yogurt

½ cup pure orange juice

1 tablespoon fresh-ground ginger

WHAT YOU DO

1. Chop the apple into coarse pieces and freeze.

2. Combine ingredients except for ginger in blender. Blend on medium for 30 seconds, or until smooth.

3. Add ginger, and blend on medium for 15 seconds.

Eyes Have It! Smoothie

DR. PEEPERS SAYS YOU NEED TO LOAD UP on vitamin C, carotenoids, and bioflavonoids if you want to steer clear of cataracts, macular degeneration, and other eye disorders. So why not get the whole bundle of nutrients in one single-serving shake? See what I mean?

WHAT YOU NEED

1 small carrot

½ red bell pepper

½ cup tomato juice

3 tablespoons fat-free sour cream

1 tablespoon lemon juice

WHAT YOU DO

1. Scrub carrot and wash pepper. Chop them into coarse pieces.

2. Blend carrot and red pepper on high for three 2-second bursts.

3. Add remaining ingredients to blender and blend on medium for 10 seconds. Blend on high for 1 minute or until smooth.

Immunity Booster

AFTER THEY REBUILT HIM, THEY GAVE THE SIX- million-dollar man this smoothie twice a week. It kept him in the pink of health, and although the techno geeks will say it's the bionics that had him running sixty miles an hour, we're betting it was the spirulina-laced health fuel.

WHAT YOU NEED

1 cup coarsely chopped papaya

½ cup coarsely chopped honeydew melon

½ cup orange juice

½ cup water

¼ cup chopped cantaloupe, frozen

¼ banana, chopped and frozen

½ teaspoon orange zest

½ teaspoon honey

½ teaspoon spirulina extract

1 125-milligram soft-gel capsule of echinacea

WHAT YOU DO

1. Combine all ingredients in blender and blend on low for 5 seconds, or until chunks of fruit break down.

2. Blend on high for 1 to 2 minutes, or until smooth.

Digestion Suggestion

THIS MAY COME AS A SURPRISE—YOUR digestive system is not a garbage disposal. Just because your tongue loves something, doesn't mean it plays well beyond the throat. Do the system a favor. Give it some smooth, gentle, nutrient-rich goodness to keep your stomach happy too.

WHAT YOU NEED

½ teaspoon flaxseed

1 tablespoon old-fashioned oats

½ tablespoon wheat germ

½ cup plain nonfat yogurt

½ teaspoon cinnamon

½ teaspoon pure vanilla extract

2 pitted prunes

2 teaspoons raisins

¼ cup water

WHAT YOU DO

1. Combine flaxseed, oats, and wheat germ in blender. Blend on high for two 2-second bursts.

2. Add remaining ingredients. Blend on low for 10 seconds, then blend on high for 1 minute.

Liquid vim and vigor

Metric Equivalencies

Liquid Equivalencies

CUSTOMARY	METRIC
¼ teaspoon	1.25 milliliters
½ teaspoon	2.5 milliliters
1 teaspoon	5 milliliters
1 tablespoon	15 milliliters
1 fluid ounce	30 milliliters
¼ cup	60 milliliters
⅓ cup	80 milliliters
½ cup	120 milliliters
1 cup	240 milliliters
1 pint (2 cups)	480 milliliters
1 quart (4 cups)	960 milliliters (.96 liter)
1 gallon (4 quarts)	3.84 liters

Dry Measure Equivalencies

CUSTOMARY	METRIC
1 ounce (by weight)	28 grams
¼ pound (4 ounces)	114 grams
1 pound (16 ounces)	454 grams
2.2 pounds	1 kilogram (1,000 grams)

Oven Temperature Equivalencies

DESCRIPTION	°FAHRENHEIT	°CELSIUS
Cool	200	90
Very slow	250	120
Slow	300–325	150–160
Moderately slow	325–350	160–180
Moderate	350–375	180–190
Moderately hot	375–400	190–200
Hot	400–450	200–230
Very hot	450–500	230–260

Index

INDEX

INDEX

Index

INDEX